D0084854

MERIT, MEANING, and HUMAN BONDAGE

MERIT, MEANING, and HUMAN BONDAGE

An Essay on Free Will

◆

Nomy Arpaly

WITHDRAWN

PRINCETON UNIVERSITY PRESS

PRINCETON AND OXFORD

BOWLING GREEN STATE
UNIVERSITY LIBRARY

Copyright © 2006 by Princeton University Press
Published by Princeton University Press, 41 William Street, Princeton, New Jersey 08540
In the United Kingdom: Princeton University Press,
3 Market Place, Woodstock, Oxfordshire OX20 ISY

All Rights Reserved

Arpaly, Nomy.
Merit, meaning, and human bondage : an essay
on free will / Nomy Arpaly.
p.   cm.
Includes bibliographical references and index.
ISBN-13: 978-0-691-12433-9 (cl : alk. paper)
ISBN-10: 0-691-12433-7 (cl : alk. paper)
1. Free will and determinism. I. Title.
BJ1461.A77 2006
123'.5—dc22   2005056499

British Library Cataloging-in-Publication Data is available

This book has been composed in Jansen and Centaur Display

Printed on acid-free paper. ∞

pup.princeton.edu

Printed in the United States of America

1   3   5   7   9   10   8   6   4   2

Contents

Acknowledgments

I WOULD LIKE TO THANK the following persons who bear no moral responsibility nor are blameworthy for this work:

David Estlund, who in our philosophical conversations often pointed the way to reflective equilibrium, which is doubly appreciated given the fact that this is the only kind of equilibrium I have any chance of reaching. Vicki Prickett, the Queen of Qualia and the Fairy of Funk, for her keen observations. Jason D'Cruz for doing Canada proud. Jamie Dreier, well known espresso-vist and the world's foremost meta-meta-ethicist, for stimulating my brain. Jonathan Schaffer, who answered my questions about causation and rocks (and who rocks). Michael McKenna, fellow *Tour de France* follower, for leading me up some fairly technical climbs. Arthur Applbaum, for long conversations and for introducing the expression "cheap will" (a few months later, an e-mail entitled "Free Will" was regarded by my computer as spam, so if you want to write to me, be careful with words like "free"). Dennis Thompson, for some great points and early encouragement. Al Mele, a free agent, for showing me where the action is. David Brendel, for contributing a psychiatrist's perspective without trying to cure me of anything. Ernest Sosa for taking some time to read my work so thoughtfully. My colleagues at the philosophy department at Brown University for providing a wonderful environment. Peter Railton, Steven Darwall, David Velleman, Elizabeth Anderson, Michael Bratman, Sarah Buss, the delightfully demonic Soraya Golop, and a lively crowd at the University of Michigan, for asking good questions. My two anonymous referees (especially if you are who I think you are) for their unusually thoughtful reports. Perry Mandanis, for help, faith, hope, and his cell phone number. Tim Schroeder—all words fail me here, with the partial exception of these.

To all people who faintly recognize themselves in my fictional examples: I do hope you forgive me.

MERIT, MEANING, AND HUMAN BONDAGE

Introduction

In *How to Win Friends and Influence People*, Dale Carnegie suggests that when trying to get an angry person to change her ways, you can improve the situation immediately by telling the person something along the lines of, "I understand your position. If I were in your shoes, I would want exactly the same thing." In case the reader is concerned that this might be a bald untruth, Carnegie offers the assurance that following this policy never involves lying. After all, if you had your interlocutor's genetic makeup and life experience, you would act, and think, exactly like her. The only reason that you are not a rattlesnake, Carnegie says by way of example, is that your parents were not rattlesnakes.

There is something tricky about the way Carnegie uses his analogy. The situation Carnegie has in mind is something like this: John is mad at me because I sent him a mistaken report, and were I sent a mistaken report, I would also have been mad. Being sent a mistaken report is a circumstance. On the other hand, being born to rattlesnakes is not the sort of thing that we ordinarily call a 'circumstance'. There are things I would do in some circumstances and things a rattlesnake would do in the same circumstances. We might say, "If I were a rattlesnake, I would enjoy this weather," but this is, generally, saying that if I were a different individual (in this case, a very different one, from a different species, genus, family, order, and class), I would enjoy being in the same circumstances (very hot weather) that I (a human being named 'Nomy Arpaly') am in. At other times, we might use "if I were a rattlesnake" to mean "if I had some qualities the rattlesnake has"—for example, tolerating very hot weather. Tolerating very hot weather can be naturally treated as a circumstance. Similarly, I can say, "If I were Russell, I would itemize deductions on my tax return," but mean, essentially, "If I had Russell's accounting skills, I would itemize deductions on my tax return." Having accounting skills is usually treated as a circumstance, but being Russell is not.[1]

---

[1] I am assuming that simply acquiring the heat tolerance of rattlesnake or taking an accounting course would not, jokes and hyperboles aside, put my personal identity at risk.

Those of us who think that determinism[2] poses no problem for moral responsibility, praiseworthiness, or blameworthiness are likely to hold, with commonsense thinking about circumstances and against Carnegie, that at some point, identification with the blamed person's point of view can go too far: if we interpret being in a person's circumstances so broadly as to include all of the person's beliefs and desires and circumstances and so on, eventually we will simply be saying that if we were exactly like him then we would act exactly as he does, which is no more interesting than the claim that if my parents were rattlesnakes I would be one as well. I might exempt a person from blame if I were to discover, say, that he was under duress, and explain it by saying, "If I were in the same circumstances, I would have acted in the same way." But what we mean by that is something like "If I, or you, or other people who are fairly decent and have a reasonable concern for the good and the right, were in the same circumstances, we would act the same way. Of course, in more comfortable circumstances, only a wicked person would act in this manner, but these were not comfortable circumstances." In other words, even if one is a creature of circumstances, there must be some point at which the creature is treated as separate from the circumstances that created her. Your parents might have created a saint, a person who is full of good will for his fellow human beings, while your neighbor's parents created a monster, a person who wants to do nothing but hurt her fellow human beings. But now that the creating has been done, you and your neighbor are full-blown moral agents, and you are a saint and she is a monster, which means that you and she would choose to act quite differently in what can legitimately be called "the same circumstances." After all, circumstances created both me and the rattlesnake, and still I am I and the rattlesnake is a rattlesnake. The rattlesnake and I are not comparable agents, subject to differing fortunes only because of fate and circumstance.

Some find this type of argument compelling, and some do not. Those who are not convinced might point out that while we hold people blameworthy or praiseworthy for their actions, even those of us who, like most nonphilosophers, are willing to talk about nonhuman animals acting do not hold them morally praiseworthy or blameworthy for their actions. We would not make this distinction between human and nonhuman actions,

---

[2] Throughout this work I will talk about determinism as though the doctrine were well known and unproblematic, but of course there is a literature on understanding just what determinism amounts to, and it is complex and interesting in its own right. Nothing I say, however, will prejudge the correct understanding of determinism.

one might continue, if we did not believe, rightly or wrongly, that there is some way in which human beings are quite different from other animals. It is not at all reassuring to compare the thought that if I had Hitler's genes and environment, I would be evil to the thought that if my parents were rattlesnakes I would be a rattlesnake, because our belief that people are blameworthy or praiseworthy is based on the assumption that people are not, in this way, like rattlesnakes. It is true that an individual rattlesnake is different from the parents that gave birth to it, but from human beings we expect an additional kind of independence or individuality which a snake cannot have. Had I been in Hitler's exact genetic and environmental circumstances, I might still not have chosen to act as he did, some think. Or, if it turns out that I am as much a creature of circumstance as the rattlesnake, then I am somehow demoted, a thing instead of a person, an object instead of a subject. If we are all like rattlesnakes in a relevant sense, then some unique feature of human beings turns out to be an illusion—and with it, moral responsibility.

And perhaps not only moral responsibility: consider, for example, types of admiration other than the moral. I admire Lance Armstrong, and one of the things for which I admire him is the impressive drive and single-minded determination through which, despite much disbelief and discouragement, he turned himself into the world's greatest cyclist, even after cancer had nearly killed him. If Armstrong's achievements were merely the result of his being a superhuman physical prodigy from birth, I would not be quite as impressed: his excellence would seem more a matter of luck than of personal grit. I would still be impressed by the way he accelerates uphill with seeming effortlessness, but this seeming effortlessness means a lot more to me knowing that it is the result of a truly astounding effort. What, however, if determinism turned out to be true? Would that mean that suddenly we would have to treat such qualities as drive and determination as pure matters of luck, on a par with such things as being born a physical prodigy, and therefore no more significant?

Again, some people would think that the answer is obviously "yes," while others would ask "Why? It's still *his* drive and *his* determination. If he did not have them, he would be a different individual. And naturally, a different individual would not do remotely as well under the same circumstance, because a different individual wouldn't have had the spirit."

The same type of disagreement arises even when it comes to types of merit or value that one would not automatically associate with will or motivation. Those who fear that, if determinism is true, things like virtue and things like ambition are matters of luck, can equally fear that many other things are a matter of luck, things like love, or like intellectual and artistic talents. Presumably some of us think so already, judging by the fact that even atheists use terms like 'artistic gifts,' without being disturbed. But reading Oliver Sacks's book *The Man Who Mistook His Wife for a Hat* might make us wonder whether we perhaps ought to be disturbed by the specter of artistic or intellectual determination. Sacks (1987, chap. 1) describes a person—the man after whom the book is named—who has been an amateur painter for years, and whose wife explains to Sacks that her husband has entered a new artistic phase, characterized by less realism and more abstraction. Sacks, however, knows that the man has a brain tumor that severely disturbs his grasp of the visual world while making it the case that the patient himself is not aware that anything about his visual perception has gone amiss. Knowing this, the man's embrace of abstract painting does not seem like an artistic phase anymore: it looks like something that, unbeknownst to him, the tumor has caused him to do. If determinism is true, is all art like that? Does it mean its meaning is lost? The same questions have been asked about love and about intellectual achievements. If determinism is true, is a person's love of you no more than a pleasant mental illness? Is it just luck that someone happened to come up with a mathematical theorem?

Here is where our intuitions get even more complicated. Many artists, lovers, and intellectuals have proudly declared that they never chose their loves, artworks, or insights. "The book had to be written," says the writer or poet. "*Exactly* this book had to be written." "I don't like her work," an artist might say of her fellow artist. "It seems so . . . *willed*." "It *had* to be you!" says the romantic lover. "I *can't help* falling in love with you." Mathematicians have been known to say that the truth imposed itself on them or showed itself to them in a dream. And so on. All of these people seem to find it a point of pride that, in some way or another, they did not choose their meaning-creating life moments, but that these moments "chose them." And while we think about that, we might recall that sometimes even moral admiration uses the language of what I will call *romantic necessity*. "I cannot tell a lie," says the young George Washington in the famous if apocryphal story, and we assume he cannot because he is too virtuous to do otherwise. And here too one can mention Dennett's (1984, chap. 6) famous example: the case of Martin Luther declaring, as he risks his life for his principles, "Here I stand, I can do no other." How does it happen that in some cases we see necessity as a demeaning, dehumanizing thing, while at other times we present it as admirable, even ennobling?

There are many reasons to be interested in the philosophical debate over the possible significance of determinism, and, I suspect, many reasons for which people actually participate in it. My own interest in the question stems from my interest in a broader question: if it turns out that human beings are natural entities, just as subject to the laws of nature as anything else, is there anything to regret about this state of affairs? Suppose it turns out that determinism is true, and that everything, including human beings, is part of a deterministic natural world: is there anything about this state for one to be sorry about?

The answer I wish to sketch is bittersweet. I will argue that unless one is ready to defend some problematic positions about the mind-body problem, there is no reason to think that determinism is incompatible with the existence of moral praiseworthiness and blameworthiness, or with the existence of meaningful love, art, science, or other reasons to admire people. I say "existence" partially because my view is not based on Peter Strawson's (1962) idea of the reactive attitudes. I do not only think that in a deterministic world, we would still be rational to blame people or to love them. They would, in a stronger sense, merit the blame or the love. However, there is still something that we do not have in a deterministic setting, and that thing is something that can with full justice be called 'freedom'. Some of us wish, understandably, for a sort of control or command, if not of our fates, then at least of our own mental states, beliefs, desires, concerns, values, emotions, intentions, and so on. We want to be able not only to do what we want, but also to want only things that we choose to want. We want, in a way, to be able to decide who to be. In a deterministic setting, I will argue, freedom of this sort is the spiritual equivalent of the ability to pick oneself up (literally!) by one's own bootstraps or to find the secret of perpetual motion: an impossibility, and yet something that a sensible person might well wish for, even, in some circumstances, desperately.

That we often wish for an impossible freedom is, I think, part of what makes the human condition uncomfortable at best and tragic at worst, but uncomfortable or even tragic lives are by no means any less meaningful, and the human condition is still very unlike the condition of the rattlesnake. The difference between us and the rattlesnake is not in freedom but in the ability to *respond to reasons* (including, but not limited to, moral reasons). An incompatibilist might argue that reason responsiveness *requires* freedom, and so if we do not have freedom, we do not have reason responsiveness. Compatibilists might argue that essentially, reason responsiveness *just is* freedom, and so if we have it, we have freedom, and we need not find anything at all uncomfortable with the idea of determinism. In this respect, both the compatibilist and the incompatibilist would be mistaken. Some things, like my belief that two and two equal four, are both reason responsive and yet not free, and in fact, seeing reason responsiveness in terms of freedom obscures some of its important features. In a deterministic setting, we would be reason responsive, but not free. We would still have meaningful lives and produce meaningful achievements, and we would still be morally praiseworthy or blameworthy for our actions, but it would not be unreasonable for us to regret the absence of freedom. When Luther cried "Here I stand, I can do no other," he was not shrugging off moral responsibility, nor was he denying the meaningfulness of his quest. However, it is not unreasonable to imagine him saying to his image in the mirror, "Alas, I can do no other." In fact, tradition provides us with a fuller version of Luther's statement: "Here I stand, I can do no other. *God help me!*"

In the pages to come, chapter 1 sketches a theory of moral praiseworthiness and blameworthiness in which their existence is compatible with a world in which we cannot do otherwise. The theory does not rely on the reactive attitudes because, as I will argue, the incompatibilist is right when she demands an account not only of the reasons we might have to praise and blame people in a deterministic world, but an account of what might make people truly blameworthy or praiseworthy in a deterministic world independently of our practices. Strawson was wrong to treat the question of whether people are truly praise- or blameworthy as equivalent to the question of whether we have good reason to embrace our reactive attitudes: we have a reason to praise the person who says, "Praise me, or I'll kill you all!" but this is not a person who is praise*worthy*. Taking its cue from my account of moral worth in *Unprincipled Virtue* (Arpaly 2003), my account of moral responsibility will rely on notions of good will and ill will, moral concern, and moral indifference. On my account, to have these qualities of will is to respond to moral reasons. [3]

Building a compatibilist theory of moral praise- and blameworthiness on the notion of response to moral reasons raises an absolutely central question: Can there really be responsiveness to reasons in a deterministic

---

[3] My view is similar to the view of Fischer and Ravizza (1998) in the following respects: it allows for "semicompatibilism"—compatibilism about moral responsibility that does not depend on compatibilism about freedom, and it presupposes an important role for the notion of reason-responsiveness. It is different from theirs in that my view not only does not depend on a concept of freedom but also has no fundamental place for a concept of control, and in other ways that I hope will become apparent.

world? Chapter 2 takes on this question directly, and comes to the conclusion that if there is an incompatibility between determinism and reason responsiveness, then there are necessarily flaws in standard materialistic accounts of mental causation in which mental content plays an important role. While not wading far into this debate, I have more confidence in the materialistic philosophers of mind than in the incompatibilist intuitions that challenge them, and so am left with some confidence in the positive sketch I give of reason responsiveness in a deterministic world. In the course of arguing for this, I tackle the topic of romantic necessity raised earlier—the fact that we sometimes think it a wonderful thing that once two people met, their love *had* to happen, or that an artist's doing a particular sort of work was *inevitable*, while at other times we take to be a depressing, sobering thought that one's love or art is the result of an inevitable causal process. I sort out the sorts of responses to the world that leave meaning intact and distinguish them from those that do not.

At this point, my positive project has been largely completed. I have offered a theory of what it is to be praiseworthy or blameworthy that relies on responsiveness to moral reasons, and shown that reason responsiveness in general is compatible with determinism, so long as standard materialist theories of mind can make good on some of their most basic commitments. But this sort of positive theorizing will inevitably leave many incompatibilists unsatisfied. Admiring much of what other philosophers have said about the compatibility of determinism and meaningfulness (in both moral and nonmoral domains), and having made some particular arguments on this topic myself (Arpaly 2002), I have elected not to spend this work going over familiar arguments and puzzle cases in detail. Instead, I use chapter 3 to strike out in a somewhat different direction in attempting to answer the critics. If there is a fundamental intuition driving incompatibilism about moral responsibility, it is the idea that 'ought' implies 'can', and that in a deterministic universe, there is no appropriate sense in which one can do what one does not. Chapter 3 attacks this fundamental intuition directly, arguing that 'ought' does not imply 'can'. The argument takes us into another corner of reason responsiveness: that of responsiveness to epistemic reasons. While epistemic norms clearly exist, responding to epistemic reasons is never a matter of choice, and so the connection between 'ought' and ability is not as so often conceived. In the course of this discussion, I make clear the difference between freedom and reason-responsiveness, a difference compatibilists tend to overlook as much as incompatibilists. I also explore further what it is that we mean by 'freedom', looking for clues in the patterns which pre-theoretical (or, at least, undergraduate classroom) disagreements about free will tend to follow. This is followed by an inter-lude of sorts in which I discuss examples involving induced beliefs and desires (such as beliefs and desires induced by nefarious neurosurgeons).

In the final chapter, chapter 4, I argue that despite all of the above, there is still something sad about our being as much a part of nature as the rattle-snake. Of course, how sad one should be about it depends on many things—some of us seem to crave freedom more than others—but compati-bilists about responsibility, reason-responsiveness, and meaning in life stretch their luck when they suggest that reason responsiveness gives us all the freedom we want. I will argue that those who see freedom in the "right" kind of causation—who argue, for example, that if you are acting out of your own deepest values, then you are essentially free—are mistaken, in that what they offer are only free will substitutes, agreeable to some people under some circumstances but not to others. In the course of this, I will defend the view that there is a way in which it *does* sometimes make sense to wish for the impossible, or at least to regret that it does not obtain.

When I was beginning this project, Arthur Applbaum of the Center for Ethics and the Professions at Harvard asked me what I was working on. I said, "Free will." To that he replied, "Free will? Surely you mean *cheap* will. Nothing is *free* in this world." All in all, I think he is right, but I nonetheless aim to show that the absence of truly free will does not cheapen our lives.

I

Praise and Blame: Toward a New Compatibilism

Punishing a person is an action: it is something one *does*. Blaming a person is *not* an action—I might blame Brutus for the death of Caesar without doing anything—though the verb *to blame* can also be used to refer to the act of notifying someone that you blame a person.

The observation is hardly new, yet philosophers tend to dismiss the difference between blaming and punishing or remonstrating; we discuss whether it is fair to blame a person as if the question were equivalent to the question of whether it is fair to punish the person. This is a category mistake. The primary sense in which I can be fair or unfair in blaming someone is the sense in which believing that Ron is an idiot might be fair if Ron is an idiot and unfair if Ron is not. The primary sense in which I can be fair or unfair in punishing someone is the sense in which my calling Ron an idiot might be fair if he has just called me a moron and unfair if he has never been rude to me.[1]

Appropriate attention to this distinction opens the way to a new kind of compatibilist theory of moral praiseworthiness and blameworthiness. Neither freedom nor resentment plays a major role in the view I shall sketch here of moral praiseworthiness and blameworthiness, nor does it involve the concept of a reactive attitude separate from the objective one, yet curiously it owes a great deal to the work of Peter Strawson.

Warrant and Desirability

An action can be desirable or undesirable. An action is desirable if it ought to be performed (or to the extent that it would be better to perform it), and it can be desirable for moral reasons, for prudential reasons, for aesthetic

---

[1] For the opposing view see for example J. Wallace 1994.

reasons, or any other kind of reason. For beliefs, and certain other attitudes, there exists the further question of *warrant*. There are many ways in which the word *warrant* is used. I use it here in a broad sense, to refer to the extent to which the belief or attitude reflects the facts.[2]

The distinction is a straightforward one. If I tell a student that her fear of the exam is silly because she is well versed in the material, I tell her that her fear is *unwarranted*. If, on the other hand, I tell her that it would be wise to eradicate her fear because fearless students concentrate better and get better grades, or because courage is a virtue, then I am merely telling her that her fear is *undesirable*. It might be a sign of good parenthood for a father to be somewhat unrealistically worried about his talented daughter's chances in the world (perhaps because, in some types of people, such worry is the inevitable result of loving concern). If so, the father's worries are *desirable*—morally desirable, even—but are also *unwarranted*, however endearing. Pascal's wager is an argument for the *desirability* of believing in God, while the ontological argument tries to establish that belief in God is *warranted*. And so on.

Some compatibilists have caused frustration in their incompatibilist interlocutors exactly because they fail to respect the distinction between desirability and warrant.[3] Asked if anyone is blameworthy in a deterministic world, some philosophers will say that whether determinism is true or not, some people ought to be blamed, or that at least our current habit of blaming them ought not to be tinkered with. This amounts to saying that blaming is desirable. The incompatibilist, however, wants to know whether, in a deterministic world, blame is ever warranted, and being told that it is desirable is neither here nor there as far as he is concerned. He might very well agree that we ought to continue blaming people, and still wonder if said people are *really* blameworthy or whether we should merely *pretend* that they are, act *as if* they are, take a sort of *Pascal's wager* on the uplifting belief that they are, or refrain from upsetting our natural collective *illusion* or *delusion* that they are.[4]

---

[2] It might be more accurate to say that beliefs are warranted, not to the extent that they reflect the facts, but to the extent that they reflect the evidence available to me, or perhaps to the extent that they are reliably produced. But to sort out this matter is to sort out the nature of warranted belief, and that is not the subject of the present work. Accordingly, in this book I stick to the clear, if overly simplistic, notion of reflecting the facts.

[3] Compare Susan Wolf, "The Importance of Free Will" (1993a).

[4] See Wolf 1993a.

Some, most notably J.J.C. Smart, declare that whether people are "really" blameworthy, in addition to being such that it is desirable to blame them, is a pseudoproblem (Smart 1973). On this view, blame is just not the sort of thing that has warrant, only desirability. Saying that a person is blameworthy for something is simply saying that a person ought to be blamed for it. While Smart's view has been attacked in many ways, he has rarely been attacked for his claim that a blameworthy person is simply a person whom it is morally desirable to blame. Smart is generally attacked for his *further* claim that a utility calculus is the correct way to determine whom it is morally desirable to blame, a claim that is not our concern here. Our concern is with the claim that blame is the sort of thing that can only be desirable or undesirable, required or not required or forbidden, like an action, rather than being warranted or unwarranted, like a belief. The proponent of this claim might challenge the incompatibilist by asking what, exactly, he is doubting when he wonders if blame is ever "warranted," if he is not simply doubting its desirability. Does he doubt that people cheat, steal, and kill? Does he doubt that cheating, stealing, and killing are morally wrong? Surely he does not: people do bad things, whether they are deterministically caused to do so or not. If the incompatibilist does not doubt that people do bad things and that sometimes they ought to be blamed for these things, what else does he need? Perhaps the incompatibilist has the idea that blameworthy actions cause something like a "yellow stain on the soul" (Smart 1973, 52).

In response, the incompatibilist could appeal to the observation with which we started—that blame is not an action—and say that Smart is talking not of blame, but of the actions commonly associated with blame: punishment, reproach, and the like. It is possible to agree that these actions are morally desirable (or required) actions while worrying whether, given determinism, blame can be warranted or not.

A philosopher seeking to answer the incompatibilist might at this point turn to Peter Strawson's (1962) observation that our worries about determinism and blame do not concern merely, or even mostly, the courts of law, but the very fabric of our lives. Strawson shifts our attention from the actions traditionally associated with blame, such as punishing, toward emotions and feelings commonly associated with blame, such as anger, resentment, guilt, and forgiveness, which, together with related emotions associated with moral praise, such as gratitude, respect, and some kinds of love, constitute and color the relationships that make up human life. Strawson maintains that if determinism turns out to be true, not only do we have no reason to get rid of such actions as punishing and rewarding, but we

would also be ill-advised to tamper with the emotions in which such practices are rooted. It is possible to take "the reactive attitude" even if one
believes in determinism, and trying to get rid of these emotions would be
as futile, to borrow an expression from Brecht, as trying to make it rain
upward; at any rate it would be a foolish idea, as life would be impoverished
and meaningless without them.

As Susan Wolf has argued, the beauty and sophistication of Strawson's
view will not satisfy incompatibilists (Wolf 1993a). Taking the Strawsonian
explanation in, the incompatibilist might feel increasingly like the spiritual
seeker who, hoping to learn that God *exists*, is presented instead by hard
evidence to the effect that religious belief comes from a deep place in the
human heart and that rejecting it would impoverish our emotional lives.
Strawson ultimately provides evidence for the desirability of keeping not
only the practice of punishing, but also a wide set of emotions traditionally
associated with blame. There are two problems with Strawson's approach.
The smaller, though more apparent, problem is that not only is blame not
an action, blame is also not an emotion, nor a feeling, nor any set of emotions and feelings. One can blame Julius Caesar for some of his actions
without ever feeling anger, resentment, or indignation toward him. The
more serious problem is that ultimately, Strawson has simply added the
desirability of maintaining certain emotions and attitudes to the desirability
of certain actions. The incompatibilist can agree that emotions like anger
and resentment are important, but as Wolf eloquently points out, he will
take it as a reason to worry about the possibility that these desirable, central
emotions are about as warranted as a fear of spiders. Just as a fear of spiders
is unwarranted if spiders are not dangerous, anger and resentment are unwarranted unless their objects are blameworthy for their actions: really
blameworthy in the sense of *warranting* blame. Strawson might reply that
blame (or anger, resentment) is not the sort of thing that can be warranted
or not. Anger, resentment, and so on constitute the way human beings
react to other human beings whom they perceive as hostile or careless
toward them, and in this sense some things are unnatural or perverse objects for those attitudes, the way that the number nine is not a natural
object for visceral disgust. Still, the question of whether anger in general
rests on a mistake might be held to be a meaningless question to Strawson.

Incompatibilists have, by and large, not been convinced. They remain
worried that if determinism is true, blame is never warranted. Many argue
that even if all our practices and emotions are desirable in a deterministic
world, blame is only warranted if there exists contracausal freedom, agent-
caused actions, or the like. To be blameworthy for an action, according to

this view, is to have performed a morally wrong action through a contracausal or perhaps some otherwise non-deterministic choice, and if one has not made such a choice, blame is unwarranted. I think the incompatibilist is right to insist that a justification of blame should show that blame can be warranted, and the compatibilist would be wrong if she were to maintain that nothing is lost by giving up the intuitive notion that the incompatibilist's worry about determinism, echoed by many philosophy undergraduates, is meaningful rather than nonsensical. Yet I remain a compatibilist. Accordingly, I wish to provide a compatibilist's answer to the specific question of the warrant of moral praise and blame.

PRAISEWORTHINESS AND BLAMEWORTHINESS

The question of which positive appraisals of agents for their actions are warranted has not been discussed in the moral responsibility literature as often as the question of blameworthiness. It has, however, been discussed in the context of ethics, especially by Aristotle when discussing the virtues and by Immanuel Kant when he discusses moral worth. Some of the insight acquired by ethicists into the nature of praiseworthiness might throw light on the nature of both praiseworthiness and blameworthiness. Consider Kant's (*Groundwork*, 1964) prudent grocer, who prices his merchandise fairly but does so solely because a reputation for honesty tends to increase profits. One need not be a Kantian in order to acknowledge a sense in which the prudent grocer is not praiseworthy. One ought to praise him, perhaps, if that would help encourage the grocer to be honest (even Kant would not necessarily deny that), but he does not merit praise or moral admiration for his action.

One is happy the grocer does the right thing but feels it is a mere accident, for which one is not inclined to give the grocer moral credit. But what, exactly, makes it accidental? It is *not* simply the fact that the profit motive does not reliably produce moral actions. We can imagine a world in which some invisible hand makes the profit motive reliably produce morally right actions, place Kant's grocer in that world, and still not free ourselves from the sense that there is something accidental in his acting well. The salient feature of Kant's case is that the grocer's action does not stem from any responsiveness on his part to moral reasons. In pricing fairly, the grocer acts for a reason that has nothing to do with morality, or with the features of his action which make it morally right. His *reasons for action* do not correspond to the action's *right-making features*.

The grocer's tale, then, suggests what makes moral praise warranted. It is not enough that the agent take the morally right course of action; it is also necessary, so it seems, for her to do so (more or less) for the reasons which make it right. If, for example, what makes it right to give to Oxfam is the fact that doing so helps to alleviate the suffering of fellow persons, then a person is praiseworthy for giving to Oxfam only if she does so in order to alleviate the suffering of fellow persons—not if she does so in order to take advantage of a tax break. If the agent gives to Oxfam in order to alleviate the suffering of persons, then the agent gives to Oxfam out of an essentially *moral concern*. This is true whether or not she knows it or is inclined to put it that way: the important thing is whether she is concerned with that which makes actions right, not so much whether she is concerned with that which she believes makes actions right. If actions are made right by the fact that they increase utility, anyone acting for the sake of utility is acting from a moral motive; if they are made right by respecting persons, anyone acting out of respect for persons is acting from a moral motive, and so on.

Let us move from the possible motives for good action to the possible motives for bad action. A person who takes a morally wrong course of action often displays a failure to respond properly to pertinent moral reasons: I have moral reasons to tell the truth or to call 911, but nonetheless I lie to you or I fail to call 911—because, for example, it would be more convenient for me. In this case, I display a deficiency of moral concern, or a measure of moral indifference. One could say that I act wrongly despite the wrong-making features of my course of action, or despite the right-making features of the opposite course of action. Furthermore, it seems at least conceivable that sometimes an agent takes a course of action for the sake of the very features that make it wrong: for example, if what makes it wrong to strike someone is the fact that doing so would cause suffering to a fellow human being and Iago strikes someone *in order* to make a human being suffer, then he does not simply fail to respond to moral reasons but "antiresponds" to them. Unlike the person who does something wrong for the sake of love or money, the pursuit of which is not by itself immoral, the person who is cruel for its own sake acts for a reason that essentially conflicts with morality.

For brevity's sake, let us say that the person who does the right thing out of responsiveness to moral reasons does it out of *good will*, the person who does the wrong thing or fails to do the right thing out of a failure to respond to pertinent moral reasons displays *lack of good will* (or *moral indifference*), and the person who does the wrong thing or fails to do the right thing for the very reasons that make his course of action wrong displays *ill will*. Henceforth, I shall use the terms 'good will' and 'ill will' accordingly—please note that my use is distinguished both from Strawson's use, which seems to indicate simply a favorable or unfavorable disposition toward an individual, and from Kant's theory-laden use of 'good will' within his specific theory of morality and human motivation. I propose the following:

Praiseworthiness and Blameworthiness in a Nutshell

A person is praiseworthy for taking a morally right course of action out of good will and blameworthy for taking a morally wrong course of action out of lack of good will or out of ill will. Furthermore, (1) other things being equal, a person is *more* blameworthy for a given course of action if she acts out of ill will than if she merely acts out of lack of good will;[5] and (2) other things being equal, a person is *more* praiseworthy for a given good course of action the more good will she demonstrates in taking that course of action, and an agent is more blameworthy for a given bad course of action the greater the failure of good will she demonstrates in taking it, or, if applicable, the more ill will she demonstrates in taking it.[6] In that way blameworthiness comes in degrees.

Consider how this view can be applied. In ordinary circumstances, a person who does something wrong displays ill will or a failure of good will; thus, in ordinary circumstances, people are blameworthy for doing wrong things. Some circumstances, however, make it harder or easier to do certain things, and thus change the amount of good will that it takes to do the right thing or the amount of ill will or depth of indifference required to do the wrong thing, and thus change the amount of blame that a person merits for a bad course of action. Failing to return a friend's book simply because one is tied to a chair displays no failure of good will. Failing to return a friend's book because one is very depressed might show only a

---

[5] Of course, things are rarely ever equal: a person who has enough ill will to mercilessly tease her colleagues is not remotely as bad as a person who is indifferent enough to kill someone for money. See Arpaly 2003. While it is true that Nietzsche believed that one cares about you more if one bothers to develop ill will toward you as opposed to indifference, what he had in mind was presumably hating or being indifferent to an individual, not to (gasp) morality.

[6] What follows immediately concerns the question, "What it is to be blameworthy or praiseworthy?" Later in this chapter I sketch an account of what it is *to blame* a person (or to morally admire her) for an action, because I agree that there is more to blaming than believing that, in a certain case, blame is warranted.

nominal failure of good will if at all, because for the severely depressed person, the amount of good will required to bother with a minor duty is an amount of good will people usually do not have. (This is why depression excuses some minor sins, and why a person who does certain good things despite depression, like Kant's sorrowing philanthropist, shows herself to be praiseworthy more than a person who does them under ordinary circumstances—a "fair weather" philanthropist, as it were.) On the other hand, it takes a lot of ill will to commit certain serious crimes, even if one is very depressed indeed, and so ordinarily depression does not excuse these crimes.

I have argued for the quality-of-will based view of praiseworthiness and blameworthiness in detail elsewhere (Arpaly 2002) without explicit reference to the free will problem. If good will, ill will, and moral indifference can exist whether determinism is true or not, however, then this view provides us with the basis for a compatibilist account of praise and blame that allows them to be warranted, not only desirable. Facts about the agent's motivations and reasons make praise or blame warranted or unwarranted. There is no need to switch on some special stance called 'the reactive attitudes' in order to glimpse these facts. A criminal's ill will is "out there," evident whether one is a victim who is enraged by it, a therapist trying to change it, a Dostoyevskian woman who loves the criminal greatly while having no illusions about the horrible state of his soul, or a reader who finds nothing more delicious than a particularly good description of a particularly heartless murder. Similarly, there is no need to turn off some special stance called 'the reactive attitudes' in order to say that your colleague who neglected to say "hello" to you in the corridor is less blameworthy for his action than you thought he was because his mother just died, or that a schizophrenic who takes someone to be the devil come to claim her soul and throws a rock at him for that reason is probably not blameworthy. It takes no particular lack of concern for what is right to fail to notice a colleague after one has heard bad news, and throwing a rock at someone whom one mistakes for the devil due to schizophrenia is no evidence of ill will on one's part, and these facts are facts whatever one's emotional stance might be.

Before I continue, I would like to point out a further difference between my view and other views of moral responsibility in which the idea of responding to reasons plays a large role. It obviously follows from my view that for a creature to have the potential to be praiseworthy or blameworthy it needs the ability to act for reasons—and maybe pretty sophisticated forms of reasons. This is a view maintained by Fischer and Ravizza, but what I wish to do in this work is different from what Fischer and Ravizza do in theirs. Fischer and Ravizza argue that one is blameworthy or praiseworthy for an action if, roughly, the action stemmed from a reason-responsive mechanism, and their concept of a reason-responsive mechanism is based on counterfactuals: the way this mechanism would respond in different kinds of circumstances. I on the other hand maintain that you are praiseworthy or blameworthy for a specific action depending on the (actual) reasons from which you acted (or failed to act). In the next chapter, I will say a few things about how acting for reasons can be compatible with determinism, but unlike Fischer and Ravizza's, my goal is to describe what makes a person praiseworthy and blameworthy for an action: my goal is not to describe what makes a person the sort of creature that is, in principle, *capable* of incurring praise or blame. Similarly, I will later defend claims about what it means for one to act or believe for reasons, but I will not concern myself with the question of what makes a creature or a mechanism within the creature *capable* of acting for reasons. Like Fischer and Ravizza, I will be friendly to the thought that acting for reasons involves a causal chain between reason and action, but whether causal chains are analyzable in terms of counterfactuals or in other terms is a question I shall leave to metaphysicians.

SOME ADVANTAGES OF THE VIEW

Every now and again, a young, wealthy student claims in my hearing that a purely capitalistic society is always perfectly meritocratic and has no unfair inequalities in it. "Look," he says, "if a poor, black inner-city girl is as talented as I, she too can go to a good college. It all depends on her." When one points out to him that it is very hard to study when people shoot through one's windows, that it is very hard to get to a good college without having been through a good high school, and other such truisms, the young student points to someone he saw in a documentary or read about or heard about who came from an extremely disadvantaged background and nonetheless managed to get a good college education and a career in, say, law. "You see?" he says with true idealistic fervor. "It all depends on her. She has a choice. She can do it if she really wants to." At this point, I point out to him that that the disadvantaged, in order to go to a good college and law school, typically have to possess incredible qualities of character and make an enormous effort, while he, to get into the same college and law school, does not even have to "really want to" do it, much less make an enormous effort or possess a compelling character. Is this not by itself an inequality?

Some libertarian views of moral responsibility face a similar problem to the one facing my student's libertarian politics. Suppose that a person is either morally blameworthy or not so according to whether or not she acted with contracausal freedom, whether or not "she had a choice." If this is true, how are we to judge a person who neglected a duty while suffering from depression or severe anxiety? The question appears to boil down to whether or not the depressed person "had a choice," and it would seem that contracausal freedom is an either/or affair, so that the depressed person either "had a choice" or did not have a choice, and the middle is excluded. However, in cases of serious yet non-psychotic depression or anxiety it seems rather misleading to say that the sufferer "has no choice" when she neglects her duty, and equally misleading to say that she has just as much choice in the matter as a non-depressed person would have. The depressed person herself would often object both to a full-blown "insanity defense"— she is not, after all, insane—and to the claim that "it's your decision and that's all there is to it." The former would be as overdone as saying that anyone born poor in America is forced to continue to be poor until the day she dies, while the latter would be like my student claiming that the poor girl is as free as he because "if she really, really wanted to, she could get to a good college." If she "really, really" wanted to, the depressed person could do the same thing that requires very little motivation from her non-depressed counterpart, and this seems to affect the amount of blame that a course of action might warrant. It is easy to imagine a continuum of cases, from the mildly stressed to the near-suicidal, which corresponds to a continuum of blameworthiness for the same sort of action. (Naturally, when in a courtroom, we might need to puncture this continuum with cutoff points, but that does not make it any less true that our views of such people do and should follow such a continuum.) My view accounts for these matters of degree by appealing to different degrees of good will required to do the right thing under different circumstances. It is, prima facie, harder to explain such matters of degree by appealing to contracausal freedom as the thing which justifies blame, because it is non-trivial to give an account of degrees of contracausal freedom, and it is hard to calculate how much contracausal freedom can be reasonably expected against a certain amount of stress or depression. To some extent, the difficulty also exists with respect to certain nonlibertarian notions of freedom, such as hierarchical concepts of autonomy (if free action is action endorsed by your higher-order desires, for example, it seems again that freedom is an either/or affair).

This is not to say that a libertarian theory cannot have some account of strength of will. Some, like Kane (1998, chaps. 8, 9) for example, can maintain that my character and previous motives can make it more or less *probable* that I will perform some good action, and presumably they can also maintain that something like depression can change or reset the relevant probabilities. What such a theory cannot explain, at least not easily, is why we take the person who succumbed to depression to be less blameworthy than her counterpart who never had depression in the first place, and the person whose strong will allowed her to overcome depression as most praiseworthy of them all. What is it that makes an agent more or less praise/blameworthy for his action? Surely not simply the fact that the agent's history makes the action less probable or more probable.

From the point of view of the compatibilist, another advantage of my view is that it is not based on any notion of self-control. It is important to note that by a notion of self-control I mean, roughly speaking, a notion of control of self over self; not, for example, a notion of control of reasons over self. Fischer and Ravizza, Mele, myself, and others sometimes talk about self-control and mean "being guided by reasons." Being guided by reasons does not have to be the same as self-control. For example, a person may be guided by reasons the way that a heat-guided missile is guided by heat (more on this in my next chapter). Quite clearly, my account is friendly to the idea of the agent being guided by reasons. However, it does not rely on a notion of self-control that involves one part of the self (say, "reason" or "second-order preferences") controlling the other (say "appetite" or "first-order preference"). Nor does it rely on a notion of self-control in which the self, whatever that may be, controls its own mental states (as Chisholm [1978] points out). The moment you have to ask what your self is apart from your mental states, you are facing just as much of a mystery as a compatibilist as you would have as a libertarian.

Suppose a compatibilist starts his inquiry into moral praiseworthiness and blameworthiness by accepting the incompatibilist's view that we are only blameworthy for actions that are under the agent's control, and then proceeds to seek a notion of agent control that is compatible with determinism, one that does not imply that the agent could have done otherwise. Since we sometimes excuse people from blame who, in the simplest sense, performed intentional actions (the depressed person, the advanced heroin addict, and so on), the compatibilist comes to think that she needs, like the incompatibilist, a notion of control that is not simply control of the agent's mental states over her actions but also of the agent over her own desires, intentions, and the like: a notion of self-control or agent autonomy. Now, there is nothing wrong with a notion of self-control per se, and nothing particularly difficult about self-control in a deterministic world. My colleague can tell me, "You have to have more control over what you say," and in a clear sense he can be right, and the "self-control" of which I supposedly need more can probably be cashed out in such terms that make it compatible with determinism. Compatibilist accounts of self-control tend to become accounts of one part of the self controlling another, and there is nothing wrong with that, either. The problem starts when we make our notions of praise- and blameworthiness dependent on a notion of self-control, thus, in effect, postulating that some parts of a person's mind are not "the agent" and some are, or even without postulating such a neat division of the soul, that some things that the agent does are not "really her actions" while some are. It is hard to argue as to what makes a particular part of the agent deserving of the privilege of being "the agent," to find out what kind of self-control is the relevant one, and how to accommodate such questions as "If my great love is calling me to follow her, but my common sense tells me to stay, which is the real me to which I need to submit?"

My view starts with the idea that we just *are* our mental states—looking at an agent's mental states and wondering where the agent is would be like Ryle's old example of the person who looks at Oxford's many buildings and asks where the university is. My view can do with the concept of an agent most natural for the compatibilist—"simply a human being that acts," as Alfred Mele puts it in *Motivation and Agency* (2003, 216). To say that a severely manic person is not blameworthy for throwing your expensive vase onto the floor, one does not need to speculate that the vase throwing was not really her action but an action performed by her disorder, or that it was not an action at all. It is enough to point out that all the moral concern in the world short of sainthood would not have prevented a person who suffers from mania from doing something similar, while for a normal person, it takes a marked lack of moral concern to allow such an action. Cigarettes are, by some measures, as addictive as heroin, but unwilling, severe heroin addiction can be a blame-reducing condition in contexts in which a cigarette addiction is not. To explain this, there is no need to try to draw a line between irresistible desires and resistible desires, to say that a tobacco-driven action is more yours in some way, or to look at differences in the structure of the two addicts' wills. It is enough to point out that for a heavy user, heroin withdrawal amounts to torture, while cigarette withdrawal is only quite uncomfortable. It does not take great moral indifference to steal, for example, in order to escape torture, while it does take some to steal in order to escape discomfort. Thus, Ann Marlowe, in her

(1993) memoir of heroin use, *How to Stop Time*, says that had she stolen while on heroin, she would be fully blameworthy, and the reason she gives is that for her, moderate user that she was, withdrawal was only like a severe cold, and who would steal to avoid a cold?[7]

As we know very little about addictions and other mental conditions, we might be unsure as to whether and to what extent they excuse, but this uncertainty can be ameliorated by greater knowledge of the facts. I have said that my view is not based on a notion of control or self-control. This does not mean that control and self-control cannot be relevant to assessment of blameworthiness or praiseworthiness, simply that they become relevant insofar as they indicate facts about the quality of the agent's will. Nothing in my view prevents me from using the excuse of "factors beyond my control" when I am late because a flight was cancelled—if I had no control of the flight, it had nothing to do with my will either. Self-control too can be relevant, but also in an indirect way. Here is one example of the way it can matter: In *Adult ADD* (Whiteman, Novotni, and Peterson 1995) we are told of John, an ADHD sufferer, who saw a house from the window of his car, admired it, and, within a few minutes, bought it. John and his wife were not, at the time, looking for a house or thinking of moving: the house was purchased impulsively, like candy by the grocery store cash register. If John were normal—that is, if we could assume that in John, the same relationship between urge and action holds as in an ordinary person—his behavior, especially his failure to consult his wife, would indicate moral indifference to us. However, John's neurological disorder results in an astounding loss of self-control—however much he wants to, he simply does not have, in some circumstances, the ability to stop before acting, think, and implement his practical conclusion. Our ordinary assumptions about the connection between urge and action imply that if one's duty to the family budget is important enough to one, one will resist fleeting contrary urges, but these assumptions do not hold for John. Thus, his action does not show moral indifference: quite possibly, he has exactly the same amount of good will as a normal person who would drive by the house, feel a craving to live in it, sigh, and drive on. His lack of self-control exempts him from blame (if we assume that he has not, for example, knowingly refused to take his medication) in the same way that depression, nearsightedness, or being tied to a chair can exempt one from blame for some actions: by making it true that an action or inaction that ordinarily would have indicated ill will or moral indifference indicates nothing of the kind in his case.

---

[7] A similar point is made in Arpaly and Schroeder 1999.

And an appeal to this lack of self-control does not commit us in any way to such claims as "John's buying the house was not really his action."

The fact that my view is not control based also makes it unnecessary for it to avail itself of two problematic assumptions. One is the assumption that some desires are, by nature, irresistible and some are not. The other is the assumption that whenever one performs a wrong action akratically, what he is really blameworthy for is not the action but some failure to exercise self-control or develop it. Let me explain quickly why I think each of these assumptions is problematic.

The notion of irresistible desires tends to come up when a control-centered view explains why some actions should count as out of our control. To say that the notion of an irresistible desire is problematic is not to deny that some people cannot resist certain desires, but to doubt that there is such a thing as "irresistibility" that is not relative to a particular motivational set. For most people under most circumstances, the desire to avoid death is irresistible, and still this desire is resistible to a devoted soldier, a suicide bomber, a person extremely attracted to danger, or a very sad person. For many people, the desire to chat on the Internet is relatively easy to resist, but to a person who is extremely lonely, chatting on the Internet can become so irresistible that it can become something very similar to a frightening physical addiction, and just as destructive. Heroin addiction is very powerful, but people have succeeded in quitting, and there are even a few rare reports of people who managed to be moderate heroin users.[8] A universally irresistible desire would be a desire which is irresistible within any human motivational structure under all circumstances. Perhaps the desire to avoid some extreme forms of torture is such a desire, but I suspect few others are. On my view, since blame is not primarily a matter of control, one does not need to attribute an "uncontrollable," "irresistible" motive in order to say someone is exempt from blame.

On to ideas about failure to exercise or develop self-control: advocates of control-based theories of moral responsibility have explained how one can be blameworthy for actions that prima facie appear to be both blameworthy and uncontrolled—actions that the agent performs "in spite of herself" due to a strong temptation, say, or an overpowering rage—by appealing to an earlier moral fault in the agent, a failure to exercise or develop

---

[8] Ann Marlowe, in her memoir *How to Stop Time*, describes years of her life in which she used heroin regularly, but kept her consumption at a low enough level and her addiction at a mild enough stage that her white-collar job was not affected and her "heroin budget" did not increase, though the addiction was powerful enough for her life to "revolve around the drug"

self-control in the past, prior to the uncontrolled moment. Thus Velleman (1992, 464–65), in a similar case, suggests that I am blameworthy for not having exercised "vigilance" over my stray desires, and Watson (1977) suggests that I might be blameworthy for failure to develop proper self-control. Both types of explanations—failure to exercise self-control and failure to develop self-control—are problematic. To be sure, there are many occasions on which we do hold people blameworthy for failing, as it were, to check their mental brakes. Thus, the person whose wrong action is the result of procrastination might be blameworthy for deciding not to delete the games folder from her workplace computer, for choosing not to buy a day planner, or for taking on too many responsibilities. Perhaps the akratic adulterer should have refused that invitation for dinner while her husband was out of town, and perhaps the angry person, before his outburst of rage, should have taken a deep breath and counted to ten. But this is not all that we blame such agents for. After all, it is sometimes the case that no such "count to ten" measures were available to the agent. It is also sometimes the case that the agent could not be expected to know of such measures in time to use them (perhaps powerful aggressive urges have never appeared in you before, and when such an urge appears, it takes you so much by surprise that you do not notice it until you have already done some damage). There are also many cases in which the agent has already taken such measures, and in general tried as hard as she could not to follow her "outlaw" desires, but her attempts and measures fail. In many such cases, we still blame the nonautonomous adulterer, procrastinator, or angry aggressor. While some akratic sins do come down to someone having failed to "check her mental brakes" (one should have seen it coming, taken a deep breath and counted to ten) or even to develop self-control, it is rather cumbersome to have to presuppose such a story in every blameworthy action that anyone performs "in spite of herself." Is it true that all people susceptible to rage know when it is coming? What if it is your first encounter with the temptation or rage trigger, and it catches you by surprise? There are also cases in which no "count to ten" option exists, and yet we still regard the tempted or raging agent as blameworthy. In such cases, it seems to me, we are led to regard the tempted or raging agent as blameworthy exactly because the procrastinator does not care enough about the project to just work on it, because the tempted woman does not care enough about her relationship to reject an opportunity for adultery, because the

in her spare time. It is not surprising that she seems to have been, before and while taking the drug, happier and richer than a stereotypical heroin user.

raging person just really wants to emotionally or physically wound someone else. That is, in these cases our perception of quality of will, not failed
opportunities to develop self-control, is what guides moral disapprobation.

The idea that one is guilty in every case of akratic blameworthy action
of failure to develop self-control is similarly problematic. If only self-con-
trolled actions are blameworthy, the failure to develop self-control has to
be itself something that is under our control (it would not do, for example,
to blame an agent for a native weakness, on this view). How exactly was
one supposed to have developed self-control voluntarily? How often do we
knowingly perform character-building or character-ruining actions? To be
sure, occasionally we do. Mr. Tucker, a character in Christopher Buckley's
satire *The White House Mess*, knows that entering the White House is likely
to turn him into what he calls "a jerk." Yet he chooses to enter the White
House, and his moral character is in fact harmed in the ways in which he
predicted it would be. I do not doubt such decisions occur in real life.
But instances of such decisions are rare. Successful, intentional, character-
building or character-ruining actions performed by a person upon himself
are even more rare than successful New Year's resolutions. It is the exception, rather than the rule, that a person's character is substantially self-
made, which is why a self-made good character is so impressive.[9] In most
cases in which people lack self-control with respect to some of their desires
(or when they simply do not have strong enough "good" desires to combat
the "bad" ones), this weakness is primarily the result of early upbringing
and all sorts of unintentional psychological reinforcement. To the extent
that agents contribute to the creation of their weaknesses by means of their
autonomous actions, it is usually not in the straightforward way Tucker
influenced his own character. Tucker knew about the way his White House
job was likely to affect his character. Quite often, however, an agent chooses
her character-shaping actions without any knowledge of the way in which
they are likely to shape her character, and does so in circumstances in which
she could hardly be expected to know better (any parent trying to shape
the character of a child knows how hard it is to make such predictions).
One is not usually in a position to predict whether her choice of a job,
school, marriage partner, friends, or area of domicile will affect her moral
character in some fashion, not to mention the many choices which initially
appear too insignificant to fuss about. Thus, it is quite unlikely that what
nonautonomous blameworthy agents are to blame for is *always and only*
failure of character building.

---

[9] The claim that we have little control over the development of our character is made and
defended by Sher (2001).

BLAMING: THE SIGNIFICANCE OF THE MORAL EMOTIONS

I have presented a view according to which one is blameworthy if and only if one performs a wrong action out of ill will or lack of good will, and one is praiseworthy if and only if one performs a right action out of good will. What is it, then, to blame someone? The question is one that Strawsonians are especially likely to press at this point, for I have opposed my theory to that of Strawson without yet giving an account of what he calls the 'reactive attitudes', and some such account is owed if I am to convince Strawsonians to prefer my way of thinking of blame to theirs.

It is clear that, given my account, part of blaming someone (mentally) is perceiving that the person has performed a wrong action from ill will or lack of good will, and the positive moral appraisal that corresponds to honest moral praise is the perceiving of a person as having performed a right action out of good will.[10] Part of blaming and of the corresponding moral approval is epistemic or cognitive. However, perceiving ill or good will in a person's action is not enough to constitute blaming or morally admiring a person for an action. Intuitively, the person who perceives or imagines responsiveness or unresponsiveness to moral reasons in another cannot clearly morally approve of the person or blame that person unless she is "in favor" of morality at some level. True, it is possible to love a person and perceive him as blameworthy at the same time. It is also possible to admire a person for an action in some nonmoral sense while perceiving him to be blameworthy for the same action (e.g., admire Vincenzo Perugia for stealing the Mona Lisa while finding him blameworthy). It is even possible to be attracted to evil people, ever so guiltily, because of their very evil, or to have a sort of aesthetic appreciation for the very consistency or magnitude of a certain person's moral indifference (certainly the fictional Carmen and the real Marquis de Sade would be considerably less fascinating if they were not so breathtakingly morally indifferent). However, it seems strange to say that I blame a person for an action if I fully perceive it to be an expression of her ill will, but have a wholehearted positive attitude, or a complete absence of negative attitudes, toward her ill will and its expression. If we imagine the Devil smiling with pleasure as he perceives Hitler's complete heartlessness, making a note to give him a Bad Person of the Year award, it would be strange to say that the Devil blames Hitler for what he does. Likewise, if we imagine the Devil saying with disgust

---

[10] One can also, on my account, morally approve or disapprove of a person simply by perceiving good or ill will in her—hence character evaluations like "he is a jerk" or "she is a decent person."

that Nelson Mandela often responds to moral reasons, we can hardly call this praising. If a person wholeheartedly admires Carmen for being "like a force of nature"—that is, immune to qualms as she does exactly as she pleases—he is hardly blaming her, though he is certainly perceiving her moral indifference.

Something else is required. The blamer or admirer must not only recognize ill or good will, respectively; he must disapprove of the former and approve of the latter—both in general and in relation to the agent and action toward which the blame is directed. He needs to be "for" morality—that is, have a certain amount of moral concern himself. The combination in blame of perceiving lack of good will in the blamed person and caring about morality, given human nature, explains the emotions and urges associated with blaming someone.

The moral emotions, while not amounting to praise and blame, naturally stem from them, because they are the natural emotional responses of a person who cares about morality and who perceives good will or ill will in others. Consider, as an analogy, the emotion of anxiety. If my student is afraid of the exam, part of her fear is some kind of belief or perception, if only a visceral one: the belief, say, that she is likely to fail the exam. The belief alone, however, even if it is a deeply visceral or internalized belief, does not fear make. If you do not care at all, intrinsically or instrumentally, whether you fail the exam or not, then a visceral sense of impending exam failure will leave you unafraid. If you are desperately searching in your heart for an excuse to leave university and join the circus, a visceral sense of likely exam failure might fill you with hope, not fear. Caring about the exam and wanting to succeed cause the thought of failure to be painful in ways that it would never be if one were utterly indifferent to exams. In fact, hopes and fears are often potential clues to desires and concerns whose existence we have not suspected: when you discover that the thought of failing the exam makes you feel wistful rather than frightened, you wonder if you in fact wish to stay in your program of study. There are many other ways in which our concerns color our emotional lives. For example, other things being equal, caring about a sports team makes wins pleasant and losses painful. More than this: the person who cares about a team is likely to experience shame at its bad performance, pride at its good performance, anxiety when an important game approaches, despair if it turns out that a key player has been involved in a serious crime, and other such emotions which utterly baffle the person who does not possess such a concern.

Concern for morality similarly colors, other things being equal, the emotional life of the concerned agent. If I care about morality, I am likely to experience pain and frustration at the thought of immorality and ill will, joy at the thought of morality and good will. If I care about morality, the thought that I have done something wrong will tend to make me feel bad— to feel guilty. If I care about morality, my desire that people be good to one another or at least not be bad to one another is likely to lead me to painful feelings of frustration at the perception of blameworthy action in others. To the extent that anger is a moral emotion, it is made up of this painful frustration of one's desire that people respond to morality (or to a particular moral reason—say, the welfare of their fellows, fairness, etc.). It must be granted that this is rarely all there is to anger, but then anger, even very righteous indignation, is a complicated thing, and is rarely a purely moral emotion, which accounts for some of the general uneasiness or ambivalence about its place in the life of a good person. Some instances of anger can be closer to purely moral emotions than others, of course: reading a newspaper, a morally concerned citizen might become angry at the actions of a politician whose actions do not affect the concerned citizen herself in any direct way. The concerned citizen is mostly pained by the frustration of her desire that people respond to moral reasons, and her anger is mostly a response to the politician's real or imagined blameworthiness. Yet, even in this kind of case, the fact that the citizen bursts into anger when reading about bad environmental policies, say, and never bursts into anger when reading about discrimination against mentally retarded people, might mean that other factors—say, her love of natural beauty for its own sake or her aversion to certain politicians—also play a role. Once one takes account of the complexity of anger and the good, bad, and ugly things of which it is made, it is clear how some people can think that a perfectly moral person never gets angry while others think that a person who never gets angry must be an amoralist. On my account, it seems to be the case that given many people's temperaments, though perhaps not all, it is unlikely that one will have strong concern for morality without being prone to indignation. On the other hand, it also seems to be the case that, given the rarity of purely moral anger, a person who is angry very often is not very likely to be that way due an excess of moral concern, and is far more likely to either be venting morally irrelevant frustrations or simply be of stormier temperament than most. Of course, the fact that the presence of moral indignation in an agent is a sign of concern for morality does not imply anything obvious about the desirability or undesirability of displaying that indignation or acting on it.

At any rate, the person disposed to the more strictly moral forms of anger and guilt and to other moral emotions and feelings is a person who both perceives good will and ill will in self and others and who cares about morality in a way that implies a pro attitude toward good will and a con attitude, as it were, toward ill will. This is the person to whom perceptions of ill will cause sorrow and frustration while perceptions of good will in self and others encourage her. The person who cares about morality does not *always* feel indignation or sadness at bad, ill-willed actions or a gush of warm feeling at good, good-willed actions. After all, the person who cares about success on an exam will not feel fear if, for example, he is a very calm person or if he is distracted from his concern with the exam by a torrid love affair. The calm or lovelorn student might still be said to want to succeed in the exam (and so, for that matter, can the student who is asleep at this time and therefore feels nothing at all). Similarly, if a person who reads about the immoral actions of Alexander the Great feels no anger or sadness when reading, this does not entail that she does not care about morality. But a person who never feels anger or sorrow at displays of ill will, remorse for his own blameworthy action, or joy at displays of good will is either a zombie or an amoralist.

What is true of the moral emotions is also true of such things as the urge to punish people or, ideally, to convince them to change their ways. Blame is not this urge, any more than blame is anger, but the person who lays blame cares about morality, and as a result is expected, under at least some circumstances and other things being equal, to be motivated to try to make the world a morally better place.

The nature of blame and other 'reactive attitudes' having been given a theoretical characterization, it remains to say just what their significance is.

The Insignificance of the Moral Emotions

The moral emotions are indicators of concern for morality, which is in turn the attitude of the person who blames or approves. But, contrary to those who think that blameworthiness and praiseworthiness are epiphenomena of the reactive attitudes, it is the blameworthiness or praiseworthiness of the agent for her action that makes her an "appropriate" object of these emotions, and not the other way around. If we simply follow the moral emotions in order to figure out who is blameworthy and who is not, we are bound to be misguided. As I have mentioned, many different variables determine whether or not we feel, for example, fear. Even if you want to pass the exam and face probable failure, anything from your temperament to the presence of a larger menace can prevent you from fearing it;

similar factors can also cause you to feel too much fear or too little. Then there are cases in which we feel fear irrationally, or as a result of atavistic processes, or childhood traumas, or some capricious reaction of the amygdala,[11] or our fear is more proportional to the stakes than to the risks involved. In all of these cases, we are inclined to perceive something as dangerous because we fear it (or as more dangerous because we fear it more), rather than the other way around. Similarly, we might blame ourselves for something because we have been conditioned at some early age to feel guilty about it, not noticing this until caused to think about it. We might feel more gratitude toward the person who washed the dishes today for the first time than we ever feel toward the person who does it every day, whom we take for granted. One student of mine reacted to my statement that we feel more indignation toward a successful murderer than toward a would-be murderer who would have been successful if it were not for a freak accident with the words "we feel that way, but we also know that it's unfair." But if we do not happen to have the time and inclination to reflect on our judgments, excessive gratitude easily turns into an overestimation of the dishwasher's praiseworthiness, and too little resentment toward the failed murderer easily causes his blameworthiness to be forgotten. While the moral emotions are an important source of intuitions about praiseworthiness and blameworthiness, something like reflective equilibrium applies to those intuitions.

It is thus wrong to equate finding a person excused from blame with "postponing the reactive attitudes" or emotions toward her—something that you might do if you want to listen calmly to the blameworthy person's tale for therapeutic or journalistic purposes, or if you are aesthetically enjoying a movie like *Bonnie and Clyde*. But even the most sophisticated and introspective person is susceptible to mistaking the latter for the former—especially given certain varieties of normal emotional makeup. To illustrate how far we can go in making this mistake, here is what I take to be a case study involving very sophisticated people indeed.

Contrary to a common misconception, currently perpetuated by Hollywood, *Lolita* is not a story about an illicit love affair between an adult and a teenager. It is, as Nabokov put it, a case study in evil, the narrator "a vain, cruel, wretch." Humbert Humbert does start his criminal career by playing consensual flirting, then kissing games with the confused twelve-year-old Dolores (called "Lolita" only by him), who has a mild crush on him and

---

[11] See, e.g., Le Doux and Phelps 2000 for a discussion of the neuroscience of fear that gives pride of place to the amygdala.

who, it turns out, had been "debauched" by a thirteen-year-old boy. However, as soon as he turns the games into actual sex, she is disgusted and devastated. At this point, Humbert is the child's sole guardian, they are far away from anyone she knows, and she has "absolutely nowhere else to go." He keeps her prisoner for two years, in which he relentlessly forces her to have sex with him several times a day, warning her that a bleak fate awaits her if she runs away. Humbert does his best to distract us from these brute facts by regaling us with beautiful descriptions of her charm and the agony, ecstasy, and obsession her very presence induces in him. Now and then, however, the truth leaks through the narrator's point of view. For example, Humbert laments:

> She has entered my world, umber and black Humberland, with rash curiosity; she surveyed it with a shrug of amused distaste; and it seems to me now that *she was ready to turn away from it with something akin to plain repulsion. Never did she vibrate under my touch, and a strident "what d'you think you are doing" was all I got for my pains.* To the wonderland I had to offer, my fool preferred the corniest movies, the most cloying fudge. To think that between a Hamburger and a Humburger she would—invariably, with icy precision—plump for the former. There is nothing more atrociously cruel than an adored child. Did I mention the name of that milk bar I visited a moment ago? It was, of all things, the Frigid Queen. Smiling a little sadly, I dubbed her my Frigid Princess. She did not see the wistful joke. (Nabokov 1991, 166, italics mine)

Nabokov's is perhaps the best depiction of sinister self-centeredness in Western literature. Assisted by the language used by poets who portray the ladies of their hearts as "cold" and "careless" in their refusal, Humbert presents the failure of a child to be aroused by his abuse of her as "atrociously cruel." By grouping her distaste for him with her love of corny movies and fast food he invites his reader, to whom he speaks as one man of high culture to another, to shake his head at the crass American girl who displays such horrid taste in rejecting his "adoration," which by this point has been expressed in the most exquisite, intense prose (never mind that love of corny movies is forgivable in a girl of twelve in 1947). He proceeds to describe the state of bliss he enjoys while with her, enthralled as he is, despite all the bother and heartache she causes him, "despite our rows, despite her nastiness, despite all the fuss and faces that she made" (166), despite her constant bad moods (he later mentions "her sobs in the night—every night, every night—the moment I feigned sleep"). Again: the magic of language turns the natural responses of an abused child into the character flaws of a mistress, and the inflicting of unwanted attentions somehow sounds like unrequited generosity. When one adds up such details—more often than not, this happens only on a second reading—it is clear that Dolores is driven by Humbert to a state of vacant-eyed despair, and that Humbert has many opportunities to see that. The fact that he complains about Lolita's "cruelty" retrospectively, at the very time of his prison reminiscence, casts doubts on any claim he implicitly makes to being, at that time, a deeply reformed man. While Dolores is in his grasp, he occasionally has pangs of conscience ("I recall certain moments. . . . let's call them icebergs in paradise"), which last exactly until he feels aroused again.

How did Humbert manage to become, in the minds of many intelligent people who are not child molesters, a controversial lover exploited by a young vixen instead of a moral monster? Part of the answer lies in rhetorical devices analyzed by literary critics. Another part lies in psychological facts of which Nabokov is keenly aware but which one often forgets: for example, that a child abuser can be a person who abhors even the mildest verbal obscenities and that intense romantic infatuation can coexist with utter lack of concern for the well-being of its object. But much of the tendency to indulge Humbert comes from a simpler source: the fact that for some of us it is quite hard to feel pleasure and moral indignation at the same time, and Humbert's narrative is so beautiful that it rarely fails to please the overeducated reader. The reader who has difficulties feeling moral indignation and pleasure at the same time, or finds it painful, is pushed to "postpone the reactive attitudes" for the sake of the aesthetic experience—and that postponement can result in the perception of Humbert as less bad than he is. (This reaction is the mirror image of the reaction of those readers who, "reactively" angry at Humbert's badness, simply cannot see the beauty of the book.) In a way, then, the novel warns us against the very tendency to confuse "postponement" of the reactive attitudes with actual withdrawal of blame. This warning is one I think we do well to take to heart. The reactive attitudes are readily felt signs of what is morally significant, but they should not be treated as what constitutes that significance.

Constitutive Moral Luck

At this point, I have suggested a positive theory of moral praise- and blame-worthiness based on the quality of will one displays in acting, and shown its advantages as the foundation for a new compatibilism. Yet there are still many objections that can be raised to any form of compatibilism, mine included. In this work, I take there to be two main objections to my view: first, that one's will can no more be responsive to reasons in a deterministic universe than a stone is; and second, that to attempt any form of compatibilism is to violate the fundamental principle that 'ought' implies 'can'. Theories of reason responsiveness, in practical and epistemic domains, are presented in the next two chapters to answer these questions. But there are other objections likely to be raised to my view which are less fundamental but not justly ignored on that basis. In this section and the next, I deal with two of the most pressing.

One potential reason to object to my compatibilist account of praiseworthiness and blameworthiness is that it seems to entail that the world contains a certain amount of moral luck—more specifically, what Nagel has referred to as 'constitutive moral luck' (1982). If a man is born, or made, full of ill will, could he be blameworthy?

Let us first note that my account of blameworthiness and praiseworthiness holds that there is considerably less constitutive moral luck than one might first suspect, and considerably less constitutive moral luck than Nagel feared. This is because the person for whom it is harder to do the right thing might often have just as much good will as her counterpart who finds it very easy to do the right thing. If a person's congenital "bad temper" is the result of a blood-pressure problem, constant arthritis, or depression (which in some sufferers expresses itself in anger rather than sadness), my account holds that it is unfair to blame him as much as someone else who does not have that problem. After all, it takes more moral concern for this person to avoid the sort of behavior associated with "bad temper." If a person's angelic temper is nothing but a sort of timidity, or a sort of uncritical social adaptability that happens to fall on the ground of a decent society (if it fell on a different ground, she would have been the mother always baking cookies for the Hitler Jugend), my account agrees that there is nothing particularly praiseworthy about her. Of all the things that genes and environment can give a person, only good will and ill will can make her a better or worse person. Other things, like introversion or an "easygoing" nature, cannot do so, even though they can occasionally can make it easier or harder to do some morally required things. They can also, of course, color one's moral reputation a great deal, but they do so unfairly, as a combined result of the immense difficulty one has in understanding other people's motives and the human tendency to label people "nice" or "not nice" on rather scant evidence.

And many, many things can skew one's moral reputation in such a way. One is more blameworthy or praiseworthy, other things being equal, depending on one's quality of will, but other things are never equal—there are things like different background beliefs and different morally neutral desires. People can also be different in things that are neither beliefs nor desires or concerns, but which affect action. Things like habit, things like impulsivity, compulsiveness, or absentmindedness can make people with the same beliefs and desires act differently. Two people might know, for example, that the right thing to do when someone shoots a machine gun at you is to drop to the ground and have the same desire to avoid being shot, but only the one who has the right habits will actually do it. Compare good will—that is, concern for the moral—with, say, concern or love for a person. Two people might be equally loving of their romantic partners, but due to all kinds of things about their background beliefs and desires, and also about things that are neither cognitive nor conative—habits, temperament, absentmindedness or lack thereof, and so forth—their behavior would differ immensely. One of them would say "I love you" very often because she is loquacious; another would almost never say "I love you" because it would cheapen the words, or because it should go without saying, or because years of being habituated not to say what she wants are working against her. One of them will be possessive, the other one not so, because they have different levels of confidence. If your partner spends sixty hours a week working, is that a sign that he does not care anymore or a sign that he is a really hard worker? The answer seems to be a firm "it depends." Similar things make it harder to judge good will and ill will, and so in moral psychology, just as in relationship psychology, it is sometimes quite hard to figure out *how hard a person is trying.*

To recapitulate: a lot of things can make it easier or harder for you to do the right things, but only good will, ill will, and moral indifference can make you a praiseworthy or a blameworthy person. Still, sometimes it appears that genes and environment *do* give a person genuine ill will or moral indifference. Consider Robert Harris, a man described by Watson (1993). Harris is the quintessential cold-blooded murderer, who seems to actively, wholeheartedly rejoice in the suffering of his fellow human beings. This human monster, regarded as such even by his fellow death-row inmates, seems to be a product of a grotesquely bad childhood: his parents were relentless in their physical violence and emotional hostility toward him from the day of his birth, he was subjected to extremes of cruelty at a correctional school, and almost no one, it seems, showed him the affection he needed in his formative years. As a result, a person developed with no concern whatsoever, conscious or otherwise, for his fellow human beings.

Harris is all ill will and no good will: he acts for sinister reasons and is utterly unresponsive to moral reasons. Thus, it seems, an ill-will-based account of blameworthiness must hold that he is blameworthy. Yet his ill will appears not to be of his own making. Harris is thus a case of bad constitutive moral luck (of course, on my account of praiseworthiness there are cases of good moral luck as well).[12]

There are many respects in which we evaluate people's cognitive and motivational dispositions, their sensitivities and sensibilities and responsiveness to different sorts of reasons. Imagine, for example, an economics professor making the judgment that a certain student is, or would make, "a bad businessperson." He has no appreciation of economic factors and no will to succeed, she explains. This assessment is not changed if I tell her about the family circumstances that practically ensured that no desire to win or appreciation of economic factors could develop in the child that became this student. "Too bad," the instructor would insist, "but now he's a bad businessperson." A similar conversation can be imagined about other judgments, such as "She is a complete philistine. She could not care less about art and beauty. Maybe there is a way to change that, but I have not found it." On my view, because we cannot always control our own character, moral judgments such as "he is evil" must sometimes be treated in the same way. I realize that some would regard this view as counter-intuitive, and others would hold that if it is true, this is an unfortunate state of affairs, disturbing beyond the sort of unfairness involved in the fact that some of us will never be prudent, assertive, musical, or graceful. Why is this?

Naturally, one could say that if life is unfair with regard to morality, this is especially sad news because morality is more important than prudence, art, and the like. But I suspect that the difference between one who finds constitutive moral luck to be disturbing and one who finds it as trivial as "constitutive business luck" also has to do with a disagreement as to the nature of blame.[13] Some people take blame to be analogous to punishment

---

[12] Unlike Susan Wolf (1980) I hold that there is, in essence, perfect symmetry between the case of Harris and the case of a wonderful person who was raised by wonderful parents. Harris aside, when it comes to ordinary people, I suspect that the fact that we tend to be more forgiving of bad traits created by bad parents than dismissive of good traits created by good parents has to do with the Tolstoyesque fact that it takes very little for a person's moral upbringing to go wrong and a lot for it to go right.

[13] I thank Tim Scanlon for this point.

or derivative from it in some way, and treat holding someone blameworthy as analogous to holding the view that a person should be punished, or should be given something that is similar to punishment—perhaps punished in our minds, if not in our courts. I take blame to be not an inner version of a social sanction or a "practice," but a belief-like attitude, similar to fear or various kinds of esteem. Blame is not primarily something required or prohibited, like punishment, nor merely something that can be appropriate or inappropriate, the way that a brave attitude is appropriate for a soldier. It is first and foremost *warranted* or *unwarranted*, the way that my fear of getting a flu shot is warranted only if flu shots are dangerous to me. To hold someone blameworthy is not, in itself, to hold that any course of action is appropriate in regard to him, but to hold that a certain attitude toward him is epistemically rational: there was ill will, there was a wrong act, thus blame is warranted. In this way, on my view, blame is analogous to holding someone to be a bad businessman or a lousy artist. On the other hand, if one thinks that holding a person blameworthy is basically holding a certain prima facie view as to *what should be done to her*, the analogy breaks down. An egalitarian might hold that everyone, smart or stupid, musical or unmusical, graceful or ungraceful, should be treated equally, because luck makes people stupid or unmusical or ungraceful. If 'a bad (blameworthy) person' means 'a person who should be punished', and punishment is a way of treating a person more badly than one treats others, then 'Harris is blameworthy' is not at all like 'Harris is stupid'. That luck made Harris stupid is just a fact, but if 'luck made Harris bad' means that luck made Harris *a person that should be treated more badly than others*, our liberal or egalitarian intuitions are offended.

On my view, 'Harris is blameworthy' does not mean or entail 'Harris should be punished' any more than 'Harris is a bad businessman' means or entails 'Harris should be rejected from Harvard Business School'. Punishment is but one way, which is often but not always morally justified or required, to deal with blameworthy people. A full account of the complex relationship between blameworthiness and punishment is beyond the scope of this work. However, if one keeps in mind the separation between blameworthiness and the appropriateness of punishment, I think one will find that intuition supports the idea that Harris (and others like him) really is blameworthy.

One might ask: if a creature can be "born blameworthy" and it is fair to punish a person who is blameworthy, does it not follow that it is possible for a person to be born so that it is appropriate to treat him differently? My answer is: only in the way in which the fact that I was born incurably clumsy, and that it is fair not to accept clumsy people to dancing ensembles, implies that I was born so that it is appropriate to treat me differently. "Born clumsy" might imply, given the way the world is, "born so that it is fair not to accept her into a dance ensemble," but it does not follow of necessity. Similarly, "I am blameworthy" does not imply an automatic "I should be punished." It is important to distinguish here between the warrant of feelings and the fairness and desirability of actions. I argued above that it is in the nature of blameworthiness that it makes some emotions, like anger, warranted, the way that it is in the nature of great art to warrant aesthetic admiration and a good scientific theory warrants agreement. "What should I be feeling?" is usually a question of warrant, though at times the question arises as to whether or not it is desirable to take certain actions toward a feeling—encourage it, dwell on it, hide it, take fluoxetine to reduce it, and so on. "What should I do?" unlike "What should I feel?" is *always* a question about desirability. I do not doubt that if Robert Harris is blameworthy, some feelings toward him are automatically warranted. What actions should be taken against him is a different question.

Whom to punish and in what way is a question about desirability, a first-order ethical question concerning what we might do to one another and how we should deal with those who do bad things. Many considerations enter into the question: considerations of fair give-and-take, utilitarian considerations, considerations involving social contracts and the need to enforce them, considerations involving avoiding complicity in certain actions, and more. My view of blame is compatible with many real and possible theories as to the right mixture of considerations, and it is not my purpose here to construct such a theory. My view demands only the differential treatment of those who could not help but be bad when the view is combined with retributivism so pure and severe that it regards "must be punished" as an implication of "blameworthy." It is not a necessary truth that all blameworthy people should be punished, certainly if by "punishment" we refer to an institutional action (as much as you think your neighbor is blameworthy for having been rude to you, you generally don't wish the state to fine her) and even if punishment is regarded in a loose sense (in individual interactions, there are cases in which the morally ideal person will take no actions whatsoever against a blameworthy wrongdoer, though there are no cases in which anger at the blameworthy wrongdoer is unwarranted). It is not even a necessary truth that all people who should be punished are, strictly speaking, morally blameworthy—some of them are law breakers who do not appear to be immoral. (A law against having an open bottle of beer in a car or against possessing the feathers of endangered birds might be justified, as it makes it possible to better prevent drunk driving and poaching respectively, but it is easy to imagine a person breaking either law without doing anything wrong or blameworthy.) The question of a person's blameworthiness is not quite the same as the question of what would be fair to do to her, or what she deserves, and the latter question is only part of the question of what, all things considered, should be done to a person (for example: Augusto Pinochet *deserves* to be tortured and killed, but he *should be given* a stiff but torture-free prison sentence).

An incompatibilist might ask us to imagine that God sends Robert Harris to Hell after he dies, and take it to be a strong intuition that if Harris was born blameworthy or otherwise deterministically made blameworthy, then there would be something very unfair in this scenario. God punishing a person is not subject to some of the constraints to which a human society punishing a person might be subject: People who want to do such things as torture war criminals in order to give them exactly what they deserve are told by their critics that they should "leave her to Heaven" or refrain from "playing God," so we might assume, grace aside, that punishment follows more smoothly from blameworthiness in the case of divine punishment. Is it not unfair for God to punish Robert Harris if genes and environment determined his actions? But a universe that contains both God and causally determined Robert Harris is a universe in which it appears that God *created* a monster, then tormented the same monster in Hell, when he could have instead refrained from making a monster in the first place. At the very least, we have a being who could turn Harris into a better person, and does not do it. The uneasiness here comes not from the free will problem, but from the problem of evil invoked at one remove.

We shall return to the case of Robert Harris in chapter 3, and also discuss the case of the "born again Robert Harris"—the person with artificially induced will.

RESPONSIBILITY

The second objection I would like to consider to my sort of compatibilism concerns the way in which it deals with the notion of responsibility. Consider the following story, told by Peter van Inwagen (1975). A person fails to call the police, thus allowing a crime to occur that would otherwise have been prevented. Unbeknownst to him, there is a serious problem with phone service in his area, and so, had he tried to call the police, his call would have failed to come through, and the crime would have happened anyway. Is this person responsible for the fact that the police did not arrive at the crime scene? No reasonable court of law, van Inwagen submits, would say so, for the sole reason that the person in question could not have called the police. If the phone lines were in order, on the other hand, it would be reasonable to take this person to be responsible for the failure of the police to arrive.

Let us ignore for a moment any quibbles we might have with the distinction between calling the police and trying to call the police. I agree that as long as it is true that calling the police is impossible, the citizen in question is not responsible for not calling the police, even if it is true that he did not try to do so. On the other hand, whether or not calling the police was possible—even in a case in which trying to call the police was ruled out by the person being tied effectively to a chair—the mere fact that the citizen would not have called the police if he could have speaks ill of him, makes him blameworthy. The fact that the citizen was unable to (try to) call the police excuses her from having to compensate the victim's family. It does not, however, make me unjustified in feeling disgusted by her or by her response to the crime happening under her window, nor does it excuse her in the eyes of the priest to whom she confesses that she had no desire to call the police.

It is rather common to treat the phrases 'blameworthy for an action' and 'morally responsible an action' as nearly interchangeable, and it is often legitimate to use them to mean the same things. However, as the above story shows, sometimes the two terms elicit different intuitions. This is not only because 'responsibility' is sometimes used to describe a causal relationship. More importantly, 'responsibility' is often used to mean something along the lines of an obligation to "mop up after oneself," a liability to demands for recompense and punishment. It is easy to agree that the person who does not call the police should not be held responsible for the crime—he does not have a moral duty and should not have a legal duty to pay damages to the victim's family, for example. On the view I have presented "S is blameworthy" does not entail (though it can suggest) that S should be punished. In a similar way, blameworthiness in my sense does not mean that S should make amends or be put on trial. But the word *responsibility* is often used to refer to the things a person is morally or legally bound to do in the wake of something—usually his blameworthy action. Usually, but not always: a parent is responsible for his child's action, in the sense of owing recompense, even in cases in which the parent does nothing blameworthy, even in cases in which there is simply no causal link between the child's behavior and some parental neglect or bad upbringing. A leader can be responsible for an underling's actions without being blameworthy for them. And so on. I do not know if an institution can be blameworthy in any nonmetaphorical sense, but whether or not it can, even if one does not believe institutions really act, never mind show ill will, it is rather easy to see what it means for a company to be responsible, in the sense of liable, for the damage it caused even if the human being who caused the damage is no longer alive and there is not a single blameworthy individual on its payroll: it means that some people who fulfill certain functions have certain duties. It is absurd for a German who was born in the 1970s to say that she is blameworthy for the holocaust, but not obviously ridiculous of her to say that being a citizen of the country that perpetrated the holocaust in the past carries some responsibilities—that is, special obligations.

In other words, when "responsibility" intuitions and "blameworthiness" intuitions conflict, as sometimes they do, responsibility intuitions tend to be more about desirability—intuitions about what is moral to do or what the laws should be—while blameworthiness intuitions tend to be more about warrant. This is not to deny that there are other ways in which these intuitions split, but to indicate a way which has received less attention. The fact that responsibility has more to do with moral obligation, punishment, recompense, and other matters of desirability while blameworthiness is more a matter of warrant can help us to untangle a few conceptual knots.

I do not claim to have given the compatibilist a knock down argument against van Inwagen's objection, but a theory which distinguishes responsibility from blameworthiness might have to that extent a certain advantage in this regard over a theory which does not.[14] Likewise, what I said about constitutive moral luck in the previous section will hardly have convinced any incompatibilists concerned with the problem, though perhaps some compatibilists will find something to prefer in my treatment of the subject over other treatments. But both of these sections have had fairly modest goals: to sketch my preferred responses to certain problems so frequently discussed in the literature on free will that it is impossible to completely neglect them. But with these modest goals achieved, it is time to set our sights on something bigger: new arguments for the fundamental premises required for my sort of compatibilism—specifically, arguments that reason responsiveness is compatible with determinism's truth (chapter 2) and that 'ought' does not imply 'can' (chapter 3). These arguments follow.

[14] Arguably, one such theory is defended by Watson (1996) in his "Two Faces of Responsibility."

REASON RESPONSIVENESS
IN A DETERMINISTIC WORLD

INCOMPATIBILISTS AND LIBERTARIANS are commonly accused of holding views in tension with the scientific worldview. Less discussed, however, is the tension between some incompatibilist views and some facets of what might be termed the *romantic* worldview—some undercurrents in our culture that are, by and large, associated with artists, poets, and jazz singers rather than with scientists.

Consider two of the romantic's favorite topics—art and love—and begin with art. Some incompatibilists argue—or at times, take it to be an intuition—that a work of art is valuable only if free will was exercised in its creation. Thus Robert Kane, with supporting quotes from W. S. Anglin and Karl Popper, worries that Beethoven's Fifth Symphony cannot be a true manifestation of creativity, cannot be meaningful, unless it is freely written, requiring at a minimum that it be true that Beethoven could have, at that point, written a different symphony or no symphony at all (Kane 1998, 81).

Kane does not address the conflict between this claim and the romantic tradition that still plays a large role in the way artists see themselves. Artists talk with approval about books that "had to be written," of pictures that had to be painted, of works of all sorts that "chose their author." Many see their work as a necessary outcome of their lives. As Natalie Goldberg put it, "Writers end up writing about their obsessions, things that haunt them, things they can't forget, stories they carry in their bodies waiting to be released." Some describe themselves in even more passive terms. Mondrian, for example, says that "the position of the artist is humble: he is essentially a channel," and Virginia Woolf called herself "a porous vessel afloat on sensation" to which she "yields." Artists also tend to pride themselves on, rather than be ashamed of, the highly emotional or somewhat deviant mental states in which many of them work—states that are hardly the paradigm of states conducive to free action. One might also note that the adjective *willed*, when used by an art critic to describe a work of art, carries a negative connotation.

Now turn to love. Incompatibilists often say that love and friendship are only valuable if freely given, and would lose their value if it turned out that it could not have been otherwise. Romantic poets, however, often pride themselves on how little choice they had in falling in love and how helpless they have become since seeing the ladies capturing their hearts. Popular songs say things like "it had to be you," which is not all that different from "it could not have been otherwise." And it is not only poets who believe in a grand divine plan of some sort who say such things: a romantic who does not believe that the meeting of two people was "written in the stars" can still believe, and often does, that *once* these two people have met, there is no turning back. If a poet talks about love "freely given" it is usually in opposition to such things as arranged marriage and relationships into which one is pressured, not to determinism: it is not, usually, love that is "willed into being." More often than not, the romantic believes that attempts to will love directly into being (or non-being) are doomed, or that "willed" love is an ersatz love, a substitute for the real thing.

For the purposes of this discussion, I shall assume that 'freedom' means the sort of thing that Kane and other incompatibilists think it means: that is, I shall assume that for me to act freely it must be the case that I could have acted otherwise, and for me to love or write freely it must be the case that I could have loved or written otherwise. (I will likewise grant the incompatibilist's assumption that if determinism is true, I could not have done otherwise.) Using this terminology, I can only see the romantics in question as having the view that some actions and emotions that are *not* free are nonetheless valuable, even more valuable for their absence of freedom.

It is, of course, possible for a romantic to argue for an alternative notion of freedom, rather than to defend the value of actions and emotions that are not free. She might, for example, hold that if my love expresses my most authentic self, or if my love is of an objectively valuable person, or if some other condition is met, then whether or not I could have loved otherwise, there is a "deeper" sense in which I am free. This view, however, is by no means shared by all who have such intuitions as "it had to be you" or "it had to be this painting," and is no concern of mine in this chapter. What interests me is Kane's claim that freedom, defined in terms that require alternate possibilities, is necessary for such things as love and artistic creation to be valuable, and the romantic claims that seem to imply that freedom, *in the same sense*, is not necessary for certain types of love and creation to be valuable—and perhaps even makes them less valuable.

Both in the case of love and in the case of art, it is striking not only that a romantic sees herself as moved by an inevitability, but also that she *wants* to be seen that way. When it comes to love and art, then, there exists in our culture an attitude that I have elected to call 'romantic compatibilism'—a tendency to view some absences of freedom (and related passivity or inevitability) in a person's feelings or doings as dignified and worthy of pride, indicators of meaningfulness, genius, authenticity, or some other noble attributes—in stark contrast to those romantic incompatibilists who claim that only freely chosen projects can be dignified and worthy of pride.

Romantic compatibilism is not a narrow thesis espoused only in smoky coffee shops. Among philosophers, a famous example of a romantic compatibilist attitude is the one Dennett (1984, chap. 6) expresses when he brings us the image of Luther declaring, "Here I stand, I can do no other." In this case, romantic compatibilism amounts to thinking that Luther's purported ability not to do otherwise does not make his stand any less meaningful, but if anything that it actually lends it some added weight. More recently, the subject of "Luther cases" has been raised by Frankfurt and his discussion of what he calls 'volitional necessity' (1999). Whether or not we agree with Frankfurt that volitional necessity can, paradoxically, be a type of freedom or autonomy, the cases he describes involve actions about which one is tempted to be a romantic compatibilist—cases in which the fact that a person could not have done otherwise appears if anything to add to the value of her action.

Most cases of romantic compatibilism discussed in the philosophical literature are about as dramatic as Luther's, but it is worth pointing out that romantic compatibilist intuitions sometimes appear in contexts that are not as dramatic as all that. Consider the occasions on which one says with approval such things as "he can't tell a lie," "she can do no wrong," or "I just couldn't leave her in the lurch like that." The "can't" or "couldn't" is meant to imply a positive trait in the person's character. The person is so virtuous that it never occurs to him to tell a lie, or if it does, the thought triggers such an overwhelming counterreaction that he is prevented from lying. Or consider, for that matter, the person who comes to believe a truth because he is overwhelmed by evidence. Some mathematicians speak of truths "forcing themselves on them," and we do say such things as "a person as intelligent as Mary could not possibly believe in astrology."

There is a striking contrast between the romantic compatibilist attitude and the claim of the romantic incompatibilist that actions and feelings lose their meanings in a deterministic world, making us similar to "robots" or "puppets" (to use Susan Wolf's [1993a 109–18] analogies): incapable of truly falling in love, truly creating art, truly being devoted to religious ideals, truly having a conscience. At most, we can be "Chinese room"–style[1] imitations of creatures who do such things.

(A very brief detour for those concerned with the philosophy of mind: for all I know, perhaps certain robots *could* fall in love, create art, and so on; I don't mean to prejudge the issue here. But I follow convention in thinking of robots the way that incompatibilists have done. I assume only that there could be robots that would seem, at least to the casual eye, to be engaging in the right behaviors to, say, be in love, without really doing anything out of love. This much, I take it, is uncontroversial even to standard functionalists. When I talk of 'robots', then, this is the sort of robot I have in mind.)

How is it that many philosophers, including Robert Kane (1998) and Susan Wolf (1993a), see necessity as taking all the meaning out of love and art, as degrading to them, while on the other hand romantic souls claim inevitability or passivity with pride? One clue is found in the fact that only certain types of necessity are ever regarded as romantic: even extreme romantic compatibilists generally agree that some causal stories about the inevitability of love and art are demeaning and degrading. Start with love. Kane says that love, at least the best kinds thereof, is degraded if we think that our friends or lovers are "determined to love us entirely by instinct or circumstances beyond their control" (1998, 88). Talk of "instinct" and "circumstances" evokes such things as exotic sociobiological and drab sociological explanations of one's choice of love object, and a romantic would be the first to agree that such explanations degrade love. If a woman discovers that her boyfriend's love of her could not have been otherwise because all fifty-year-old men tend to be attracted to younger women, especially skinny ones, and she was the first young skinny woman who was available to that particular fifty-year-old man, it would be quite understandable if she would find the discovery demeaning, degrading, and unromantic. But the popular song's "it had to be you" suggests a different kind of story. It suggests that it had to be her because she is such a wonderful woman, and he has such good taste, that it is simply unimaginable that he would know her and not love her. *This* kind of "it couldn't have been otherwise" does not sound demeaning to the romantic compatibilist. It sounds, well, romantic. Or the song lyrics suggest that she and he are so compatible, in values and character, that it is inevitable that they be happy together: less romantic, arguably, but to many of us, far from demeaning.

---

[1] See Searle 1980.

A similar distinction can be made between two sorts of deterministic explanations of art. When Kane (1998) says that deterministic explanations demean art, he has in mind brute historicist explanations of works of art or explanations that reduce an artist's work to his childhood neuroses. If one reads, say, orthodox Freudian accounts based on the assumption that everything about an artist's work can be explained by mechanisms set in action by childhood sexuality, one can readily agree with Kane. Thus fin de siècle journalist Karl Kraus accused Freud of "reducing Grecian urns to chamber pots." The romantic who says that his art *had* to be the way it is thinks of a different story: for example, that his particular temperament (often stormy), circumstances (often complex and adverse), and abilities make him sensitive to a particular type of beauty or aesthetic truth and unable to ignore it, and that once recognized (not itself an act of will), this beauty or truth is so compelling that the artist has an overpowering desire to share it with the world. This latter sort of story holds out promise of a kind of meaningfulness that the former precludes.

Similarly, the romantic interpretation of "I can do no other" presumes a certain type of story—roughly, that Luther was so brave, so devoted to his cause, so morally outraged with the condition of the Catholic Church, so loving of God, that nothing could stop him from acting as he did, including his own fear of death. That a person "can't tell a lie" likewise only speaks well of someone in select contexts. If you cannot tell a lie because of your overly expressive face, your lack of imagination, your lousy memory, your autism, or your failure to have ever completely outgrown the sense that your parents can read your mind, it hardly counts in your favor. Those who use "can't tell a lie" as an expression of approval don't use it in such cases. Instead, they use it in cases in which, unlike most of us, you care so much about the moral value of telling the truth that, unlike people of lesser virtue, lying is just not an option for you.

Thus, the romantic compatibilist does not say that every inevitable love, inevitable work of art, or inevitable act of conscience is meaningful. She says that *some* causal stories ennoble a love, a work of art, or an act of conscience, but agrees that other causal stories can degrade love, art, or conscience just as badly as Kane and Wolf think they do. While there may be no philosopher who is a pure romantic compatibilist—no philosopher who thinks that inevitability of the right sort *ennobles*—it is still true that romantic compatibilist intuitions play a large role in the arsenal of the philosophical compatibilist, the philosopher who thinks that inevitability does not matter. Since Dennett (1984, chap. 6), "Luther cases" have been used by those who argue that what I will call 'the robot claim'—the claim that if determinism is true, we are *mere* machines—is false. Luther cases are recruited when the compatibilist attempts to show that the difference between a person and a robot is not that the robot is 'caused' and the person is not, but that human beings' mental states and actions can be causally determined by things that cannot determine the states and deeds of robots: desires, beliefs, artistic inspiration, love, religious faith, a conscience that disapproves of lying, awareness of artistic beauty, the admirable attributes of one's beloved, the despicable nature of the practice of selling divine absolution, or the moral wrongfulness of lying.

Needless to say, those who accept the robot claim are not swayed by such distinctions. Many will deny that the situations described by the romantic compatibilist involve genuine necessity (Kane, for example, holds that we assume that Luther at least chose to be the *sort* of person who feels compelled to perform his action). To the compatibilist's claim that even in a deterministic world human beings would be distinct from robots in being capable of artistic inspiration, love, or conscience, the incompatibilist who accepts the robot claim replies that nothing exists in a deterministic world that can be properly called 'love' or 'inspiration', 'conscience', or even 'belief'. Artistic beauty, the admirable attributes of one's beloved, the despicable nature of selling divine absolution, or the moral wrongfulness of lying might cause us to do things, but only in the way that an onion can cause tears or Maria Callas's voice can cause a glass to break: in a meaningless, robot-like way. At which point, the compatibilist and the robot-incompatibilist tend to stare at blankly each other, each waiting for the other to see the obvious truth of her view.

Defending the robot view is harder than it might seem, however. The robot view is essentially the view that being responsive to moral, artistic, romantic, and otherwise important reasons is not compatible with causal determinism. And though it has not been generally noticed, such a view commits one to a substantive, controversial, and probably false view regarding the mind-body problem.

Imagine an opera singer singing about love.[2] She hits a high E; as a result, a glass breaks. In this case a love song caused the glass to break but, presumably, the breaking of the glass had nothing to do with the content of the song. If the song had been about, say, frogs, the glass would have broken just the same, so long as a high E was hit at the requisite volume. In other words, though the song happened to have a certain content, the *content* of the song was not efficacious in breaking the glass. If, on the other

---

[2] The example is borrowed from Dretske (1988, 79).

hand, the song were to send a recently divorced listener into tears, the content of the song would seem to have played an important causal role in this latter incident.

Now, suppose the thought of meeting my one o'clock class fills me with dismay. If any sensible form of materialism is true, then in some way or another both my thought of meeting the class and my dismay are, or are realized by, physical states: brain states.[3] One neural state—my thought of the class—causes another neural state—my dismay. It would seem that the first brain state did not cause the second brain state in just the same way that the opera singer's song caused the glass to break. The brain state (a thought about my class) caused the other brain state (dismay) by virtue of its content, it would seem. If the thought were not about my class but about, say, frogs, it would not have elicited dismay, and this fact suggests that the content of my thought was at least part of what mattered to the causal process: the thought about my class elicited the dismay *by virtue of* its content. It should be uncontroversial that brain states—even brain states that are also mental states—can cause each other in the way that the voice of the opera singer causes the breaking of the glass. It might happen, for example, in epileptic seizures. But it appears that there are other sorts of causal events that take place in the brain as well. If all causation of one mental event by another were just like the song causing the glass to break, however, we would indeed be like robots.

The claim that there are importantly non-robotic forms of causation in the brain is one that is defended by various philosophers of mind, in various ways (see, e.g., Davidson 1980; Dretske 1988; Kim 2000). These philosophers face quite a challenge. If mental states are also physical states, how can one mental event cause another by virtue of its content? (Or, how can content have a privileged explanatory role in causal explanations involving brain states?)[4] This is the problem of content efficacy.

---

[3] Because this is not a work in the philosophy of mind, I will allow myself a certain short-hand, and will generally talk about mental states as being identical to brain states. But if the reader's preferred form of materialism is some form of functionalism, rather than identity theory, then I have no complaints, and nothing will be affected by replacing identity theory–favoring phrases with functionalism-favoring phrases.

[4] I write in general as though the problem of content efficacy were the problem of explaining how content properties could be causally efficacious, but this is not the only way philosophers of mind have regarded the problem, and is certainly not how Davidson (1980) looks at it, for instance. But these distinctions, while important, are giving me no unfair advantage in my dialectic with the defender of the robot claim, and so I will allow them to go unmentioned in general.

"How is content efficacy possible?" is not a question I will try to answer here: I leave it to philosophers of mind. But notice that the defender of the robot claim is committed to denying that the question can be answered in the way philosophers of mind generally think it can be. If determinism would leave us no more responsive to the contents of our thoughts and wishes than robots are, then the truth of determinism is incompatible with any solution to the problem of content efficacy, in spite of what philosophers of mind have generally thought. After all, a solution to the problem of content efficacy would precisely be an explanation of how it is that we are moved by *what* we think, *what* we care about, and so on, and not merely causally prodded by the existence of these mental states.

Some of the problems with explaining content efficacy have to do with difficulties in the idea of causal efficacy simpliciter. One does not want it to turn out, for example, that a world in which a demon ensures that glasses break in the presence of love songs counts as a world in which the content of love songs causes glasses to break, but deviant causal chains of this kind are a problem in general for theories of causation, and are not particular to questions of content efficacy in particular. What does it take, for example, for the weight of a rock to be efficacious in breaking a window? If one says that it is merely the truth of some simple counterfactuals, such as that the window would not have broken had the rock weighed much less, then again we can imagine a demonic world in which the counterfactual is false (the demon would have intervened to ensure that the window would have broken even though the rock weighed as little as a feather) and yet which does not strip us of the conviction that, even so, the weight of the rock (and not its color or igneous origins) caused the window's breakage when the rock struck the window. These sorts of puzzles should be left to metaphysicians, not moral psychologists. Accordingly, I will not treat any question that is raised as much by rocks as much as by mental states. All I wish to say here is that the robot claim requires that the content of our mental states is not causally efficacious, if determinism is true. That is, the robot claim requires that the puzzles challenging philosophers of mind interested in content efficacy, and perhaps all metaphysicians interested in causation, are problems that *cannot* be solved so long as determinism is held to be true. This is a serious cost to the defender of the robot claim.

How can the romantic incompatibilist respond? The truly bold romantic incompatibilist can embrace the consequences of the robot claim and begin to argue against those philosophers of mind who claim to be making progress in showing how content efficacy is possible in a deterministic world, and the profoundly lazy romantic incompatibilist can sit back and wait for philosophers of mind to announce on their own that they cannot solve the problem of content efficacy without invoking indeterminism, unlikely as this might be. I have nothing further to say to these sorts of romantic incompatibilists. But an intermediate position is likely to tempt the romantic incompatibilist: hold that philosophers of mind, although investigating something of interest, are not really investigating the right thing, and so their success is independent of the truth of romantic incompatibilism. The romantic incompatibilist can modify her position and say that while we would not be exactly like robots in a deterministic world, we would be like lower animals or very young children. In order to say that, there is no need to commit oneself to the denial of content efficacy; it is after all plausible that *some* content efficacy exists in the workings of the brains of lower animals. But human beings, unlike these animals, have the ability to *respond to reasons*, both epistemic and practical—and this, the romantic incompatibilist might argue, is the ability we lose in a determined world. She might then add that what gives meaning to the art and love of adult human beings, not to mention things like their concern for the true or the good, surely depends in some way on our ability to respond to reasons.

Further reflection on the difference between content efficacy and reason-responsiveness will show that if content efficacy exists, then there is no particular reason that the "lower animals" view is any more likely to be true than the robot claim. Reason responsiveness is compatible with determinism, whether or not freedom (properly so called) is compatible with it. I begin the argument for this claim by working to clear the ground of some old philosophical prejudices about the nature of reason that might incline one toward romantic incompatibilism; a supporting general view of reason responsiveness follows.

Talk of reason responsiveness naturally draws on notions of rationality in general, and it is here that some clarification is needed at the outset. People outside my field assume that when I say "rationality," I am referring to a state that calm, cool, and calculated people experience and very emotional ones do not, or that the same person experiences in calm moments and not in emotional moments. I have to explain to them that this is not what rationality is about. At four in the morning, in a state of emotional turmoil, a person might realize that she needs to leave her husband, and be quite rational in so concluding. At noon, in an air-conditioned room, calmly and confidently, a sleek presidential aide might reach certain conclusions regarding changes in economic policy, and her conclusions might be tragically irrational—the result of conceit or self-deception or just a tendency to make certain fallacies. While we all know this, still, the first image we see when we think of a rational person is likely to be someone calm, and so we sometimes forget that the correlation between rationality and calm is not complete. There are things in the way that moral psychologists think of rationality and of acting for reasons that can, in a similarly subtle way, make some types of reasoned actions more salient than others. And some of those make the notion of rationality or of responding to reasons look inseparable from the notion of freedom. In this section, I discuss our tendency to see rationality as a state in which some parts of the mind control (or justly govern) other parts and the tendency to think that we cannot act rationally without thinking of ourselves as free or active or in control. Both these tendencies have to do with the salience, in philosophical discussion, of rational actions that are the result of deliberation or reflection, and can be seen to be unwarranted once a broader range of examples are considered.

One thing that makes it natural to think of rationality or acting for reasons or believing for reasons as a sort of freedom is the traditional tendency to think of rational action as involving a type of control—perhaps control of the faculty of reason over the appetites or inclinations or emotions. Few contemporary philosophers hold an unmitigated faculty psychology of this sort, or any other view committed to a stark division between a "rational part" and an "irrational part" of the soul, and much of what we know about empirical psychology shows that it is unlikely to be true (Arpaly 2002, chap. 2; cf. Watson 1977). However, some of the ways in which we think about rationality philosophically are still tinged with the residue of this crude form of faculty psychology, making it natural to imagine the mind in some ways rather than others. Take, for example, the expression 'rational self-control' (or 'rational autonomy'). The expression need not mean anything more specific than the ability to act or believe for reasons—an ability of which many different accounts are possible. However, 'rational self-control' evokes the image of one part of the self controlling or ordering another part, the way one might control a dog, a horse, a car, or a slave. This makes it natural to imagine rationality as a state in which "the right part" or "the rational part" of the self is in the driver's seat, which is not so far from thinking in terms of 'reason' and 'appetite'.

This is not the only way in which to model a self controlled by rationality, a person who routinely responds to reasons. One can imagine, for example, being guided by reasons in a way that is analogous not to the way a horse is reined in by a rider, but rather to the way in which a heat-guided missile is guided by heat. The latter model fits some phenomena better than the "driver's seat" type models of being guided by reason. For a few examples, consider cases in which a person appears to be acting very much for a reason and yet does not have the prototypical experience of deliberating, perhaps because he has no time to deliberate. Consider cases in which a person does not experience himself as ordering himself to act for reasons but as struck by reason or as inexorably drawn to a conclusion. Or, consider how some things would occur to one person but not to another, because one person is better guided by reason than the other. Of course, there can be many variations on a model like this, just as there are many variations of the model of reason as charioteer, and there are probably many other ways to model the mind besides these. At this point, all I wish to point out is that such terms as 'rational self-control' can smuggle the charioteering model very early into our discussions and make us ignore other possibilities.

Similarly, consider talk of the authority of reflection (or of deliberation). Thinking of deliberation or reflection as authoritative also invokes an image of rational action as action involving one part of the mind being controlled by others—for us to act rationally, the rest of our mental states have to "obey" the authoritative "government" of deliberation or reflection. The claim that deliberation or reflection has something like authority might seem trivially true because it seems similar to the uncontested truth that rationality is normative, a truth that can also be expressed with the words "reason has authority." But if one seriously considers the possibility that 'reason' is not the name of a faculty, one cannot dismiss the possibility that the two claims are quite different.

Rationality is no doubt normative—there is clearly something wrong with acting or believing irrationally—but that does by itself entail that reflection or deliberation or something in the mind that can be called "the faculty of rationality" has any particular authority. Rationality is a system of norms, and when we have trouble figuring out what rationality requires of us, we use deliberation and reflection in an attempt to find out what it requires. Deliberation and reflection presuppose the authority of rationality rather than construct it.[5] Ideally, our deliberation and reflection successfully capture what rationality requires of us, but sometimes our deliberation or reflection itself fails us. When I say it fails us I do not mean that it gets us in trouble or results in a false belief, but rather that the *deliberation or the*

---

[5] Even if you think that the nature of our deliberation creates some norms of rationality, it is very difficult to explain how it does so without referring to some prior requirements of rationality: if, for example, you think that some actions or beliefs are ruled out because they are inconsistent with our reflective nature, you still appeal to consistency, which appears to be a requirement of rationality itself.

reflection itself fails to meet the requirements of rationality, and as a result of this—and not, say, as a result of some ignorance on our part—it does not, except by lucky coincidence, lead us to the right conclusion as to what rationality requires of us to believe or do. Consider for example the well-known scene from *Monty Python and the Holy Grail* (Gilliam 1975) in which a group of medieval people tries to decide how to find out whether the person they have captured is a witch (and thus, of course, punishable by burning):

BEDEVERE: Quiet! Quiet! Quiet! Quiet! There are ways of telling
    whether she is a witch.
VILLAGER #1: Are there?
VILLAGER #2: Ah?
VILLAGER #1: What are they?
CROWD: Tell us! Tell us! . . .
BEDEVERE: Tell me. What do you do with witches?
VILLAGER #2: Burn!
VILLAGER #1: Burn!
CROWD: Burn! Burn them up! Burn! . . .
BEDEVERE: And what do you burn apart from witches?
VILLAGER #1: More witches!
VILLAGER #3: Shh!
VILLAGER #2: Wood!
BEDEVERE: So, why do witches burn?
    [*pause*]
VILLAGER #3: B— . . . 'cause they're made of . . . wood?
BEDEVERE: Good! Heh heh.
CROWD: Oh, yeah. Oh.
BEDEVERE: So, how do we tell whether she is made of wood?
VILLAGER #1: Build a bridge out of her.
BEDEVERE: Ah, but can you not also make bridges out of stone?
VILLAGER #1: Oh, yeah.
RANDOM: Oh, yeah. True. Uhh . . .
BEDEVERE: Does wood sink in water?
VILLAGER #1: No. No.
VILLAGER #2: No, it floats! It floats!
VILLAGER #1: Throw her into the pond!
CROWD: The pond! Throw her into the pond!
BEDEVERE: What also floats in water?
VILLAGER #1: Bread!
VILLAGER #2: Apples!
VILLAGER #3: Uh, very small rocks!
VILLAGER #1: Cider!
VILLAGER #2: Uh, gra—gravy!

VILLAGER #1: Cherries!
VILLAGER #2: Mud!
VILLAGER #3: Uh, churches! Churches!
VILLAGER #2: Lead! Lead!
ARTHUR: A duck!
CROWD: Oooh.
BEDEVERE: Exactly. So, logically . . .
VILLAGER #1: If . . . she . . . weighs . . .
        the same as a duck, . . . she's made of wood.
BEDEVERE: And therefore?
VILLAGER #2: A witch!
VILLAGER #1: A witch!
CROWD: A witch! A witch! . . .

Here we have an example—in parody form—of what can happen when we reflect and deliberate but do so irrationally. Note that "irrational deliberation" or "irrational reflection" are almost never mentioned in philosophy, while "rational deliberation" and "rational reflection" are often mentioned. I do not think anyone denies that irrational reflection and irrational deliberation exist: irrational reflection is present in the work of the student who told me that "morality is a completely subjective matter and therefore it is absolutely immoral to be intolerant," while irrational deliberation is exploited by any salesperson who succeeds, without using actual lies, in maneuvering a person into buying a carpet that she does not need or a car she cannot afford. No philosopher that I know argues otherwise. However, the fact that "rational deliberation" is often mentioned but "irrational deliberation" is not contributes to the impression that deliberation and reflection constitute rationality itself, or the ultimate source of the normative force of rationality (see, e.g., Korsgaard 1996). This, in turn, encourages our tendency to see the rational person in terms of some part of the mind controlling others and makes the claim that rationality in an agent is a form of self-control appear more obvious than it is.

Related to the idea of rationality as control, but not identical to it, is the idea that in order to act for reasons, we must see ourselves as acting freely. A simple version of the argument can be formulated this way:

1. Whenever we act for reasons, we deliberate.
2. Whenever we deliberate, we see ourselves as free.

Therefore,

3. Whenever we act for reasons, we see ourselves as free.

Naturally, if it is required that we *see* ourselves as free in order to act for reasons, it still does not follow that we have to *be* free in order to act for reasons. It is also true that it is somewhat unclear what is meant by seeing yourself as free. One sense of "free" that I will not discuss here very much is the sense of "having an open future," with the attendant paradoxes involving the effects of predicting one's own decisions (deterministic predictions—or even probabilistic ones, like in the Newcomb problem!) on actually making these decisions. On this matter, I find that I have little to add to Hillary Bok's discussion (1998, 109–14). The sense of freedom I wish to discuss here, which is taken to be just as important by some philosophers (e.g., Korsgaard 1996) is the experience of "up to me," the experience of being active rather than acted upon, in control rather than controlled, which often does accompany deliberation, especially if it takes place against a background of mental states, like cravings or fears, by which one *does* feel acted upon.

I would like to mention briefly an argument that is similar to the one above but is more complex. This is the argument that derives "we must think ourselves free in order to act for reasons" from the premise "we must think ourselves free in order to *perceive* ourselves as acting for reasons" (or at the very least in order to think of ourselves as acting rationally, which is presumably something like acting for good reasons). But to derive the conclusion that one must presuppose freedom in order to act rationally, it is not enough to point out that from the first-person perspective, it is impossible, at the time of deliberation or decision, both to see yourself as acting rationally and to see yourself as lacking freedom. It is not enough because the significance of what one thinks of oneself from the first-person perspective at the time of deliberating upon future action depends on many things. For example, if it turned out that people are often mistaken at the time of action or planning about how rationally they were acting, then it would not seem to matter that much whether or not something is necessary for them in order to *see* themselves as rational. If seeing yourself as acting rationally does not have a compelling correlation with actually acting rationally, the fact that an agent at the time of agency must see herself as free in order to see herself as rational might just be a fact about the first-person perspective, analogous perhaps to the fact that whatever they think about the shape of the earth, Americans and Australians who wish to walk must, while walking, both see the sky as being above and the ground as being below. Perhaps it is little more than the fact that human beings are incapable of making a decision and predicting the decision at the very same moment. Notoriously, one can think of oneself as acting rationally while one is in fact irrational, and I have argued (Arpaly 2003) that the opposite is possible as well—one can act rationally but mistakenly think that one does not. It is also possible not to know if one is acting rationally or not ("tell me, am I crazy?").

Let us go back to the original argument, the one that relied on the premise that (1) whenever we act for reasons, we deliberate and (2) whenever we deliberate, we see ourselves as free. (1) is false and there are good reasons to doubt (2). As for (1), quite often we act for reasons without deliberation. Not only is premise (1) false, and the argument in question unsound, but, given the existence *both* of irrational deliberation *and* rational non-deliberation, the fact that something might go necessarily with deliberation does not have quite the normative significance it is taken to have: after all, that something is necessary for a process, deliberation, that is sometimes rational and sometimes is not might be a significant fact, but it does not show that the thing in question is necessary for rationality itself.

The relation between rationality and deliberation is complex, and I want to discuss it at considerable length. So I begin by first quickly casting doubt upon premise (2), that whenever we deliberate, we see ourselves as free. Even when we do deliberate, it is not always clear that we feel free. I am grateful to Vicki Prickett for the following example:

> José is overcome by grief when he learns that his wife and small daughter were killed in a car crash. At first, he is so flooded with emotion that he can barely speak a coherent sentence or do the simplest task. After a short while this near-paralysis subsides and José is able to function again (though perhaps at reduced capacity). Understandably, however, deep feelings of grief and loss persist. During the course of the next year, José's life seems to become bifurcated. On the one hand, there are the myriad mental states and behaviors relevant to the demands of daily life. José continues to go to work and performs his duties adequately. He showers, gets dressed, and eats breakfast every morning. He pays the bills, walks the dog, and so on. In addition to these long-standing routines, José has to make decisions and do unfamiliar things as well. He has to deal with funeral expenses, hospital bills, insurance claims, and so on. He has to decide what to do with his wife's and daughter's belongings. Perhaps he sells the family house and moves into a small apartment. He performs all of these tasks in a rational and deliberate manner and is conscious of doing so.

> José, like many bereaved people, might feel entirely consumed by the grieving process. Though he carries on with necessary decisions and activities, these seem to happen on autopilot. What José considers to be his essential

self is the person who is suffering from a terrible sense of loss, who is constantly remembering his loved ones, who is prone to intense feelings of sadness, anger, hopelessness, and so on. When José is acting on the basis of *this* set of mental states, he feels that it is *really him* who is acting, though these behaviors are rarely if ever deliberation-based. By contrast, when he is sensibly making decisions and taking care of his practical affairs, he feels alienated from those behaviors and mental operations. He sees deliberative trains of thought chugging along in his mind and resulting in reasonable and well-planned actions, but he is privately rather amazed that this is happening. All this rationality appears, from José's perspective, to be something cold and mechanical—a "program" his mind is running with no input from *him*. Whereas the paradigmatic Kantian agent equates the true self to the *rational will* and sees contingent psychological states as "alien forces," our grieving husband and father feels quite differently. José (perhaps in general, but certainly during this time period) sees his essential self as constituted by the contingent states disowned by the Kantian—his memories, his emotions, his attachments—and he feels alienated from his rationality and practical deliberations. José does not believe that these are "alien" in the sense that they are caused by an outside force; he knows that his deliberations are solely the workings of his own brain. Nevertheless, he has no sense of freedom regarding them. Phenomenologically, it appears to him that there is a sort of decision-making machine in his head which operates without his endorsement. He might even have explicit feelings of *not* controlling this process. We can easily imagine, for example, that José is a very deliberate and rational person by temperament and long-standing habit, and consequently his grieving is given very little outward expression. Most of his behavior continues to be the same as it ever was. Privately, however, he might very well wish that this were not the case. He might long to stop being so sensible and simply indulge his grief—engage in wild expressions of emotion, disregard prudence and morality, make foolish choices, behave *irrationally* for once—but he cannot stop the decision-making machine or control its output any more than he can voluntarily stop his heartbeat or digestion. Far from seeing himself as *free*, he sees himself as a prisoner of his own practical reason.

Turn now back to the more involved question of the truth of (1), the thesis that deliberation is required in order to act for reasons. It seems to me that, contrary to (1), we often respond to reasons, respond even to very good reasons, without deliberation. If we act for reasons without deliberation (or rationally develop beliefs without reflection), then even if it were true that every time we deliberate we see ourselves as free, it would not follow that we see ourselves as free every time we act for reasons. If deliberation is not always rational and acting without deliberation can be acting rationally, then even if it were true that we always see ourselves as free if we deliberate, that would be simply a fact about a process called 'deliberation'—not a fact about rationality.

By 'deliberation', I am referring here to conscious practical reflection. Some use the term 'deliberation' to refer to just about any process that involves inference, as opposed to more atavistic things, but some processes involving inference have a very different first-person feel from deliberation as traditionally described. In fact, there are some distinctly intelligent and inferential processes that can appear atavistic at first glance. I prefer at this point to distinguish between them and reserve the term 'deliberation' for paradigmatic, "deliberate" deliberation. This is also useful because when we ponder whether or not we see ourselves as free, or as anything else, during deliberation, it is a considerably more straightforward affair when it comes to a conscious process. José notwithstanding, it is often true that conscious reflection clearly involves a sort of seeing of oneself as free. It is considerably less obvious how we "see" ourselves when we infer things without a conscious reflective process. For the moment, let us just look at cases of reason-responsiveness without deliberation.

There are many things that we seem to do for reasons, or for good reasons, without deliberation. One of the most striking examples is what happens when we engage in fast but sophisticated linguistic behavior. A witty conversationalist, one who finds an entertaining and clever answer to every question, does not have time to deliberate upon her remarks. Yet she acts for good reasons in her choice of answers. While no deliberation is going on in the conversationalist's head, some rather complex inferences are taking place. While we might call what she has "instinct," there is quite a distance between the instinct that makes the mouse freeze in place as it hears the cry of the owl and the "instinct" that causes Oscar Wilde, having promised to make a pun on every subject, and having been asked to make a pun about the queen, to answer quickly that the queen, after all, is no subject. Oscar Wilde's reaction might be fast, and he might "hear himself" say what he is saying, unable to predict its content before he has spoken, but his quips are not the products of any atavistic mechanism.

Of course, the conversationalist is not the only example of a person who acts rationally or for reasons without deliberation. A football quarterback executing a brilliant pass (one displaying creativity and insight into the weaknesses of the defense, not merely accuracy) might simply have seen the opportunity and acted on it. For a humbler example, I can also mention an experience I once had while walking with a friend and thinking deeply about deliberation. I was congratulated for walking around a tree it seemed I was going to hit, and was forced to answer "Tree? What tree? And did I really swerve around it?" Not walking into obstacles is a sophisticated skill, and one that responds to our reasons (if I *want* to bump into things, I don't have any trouble doing so), but in my case it had clearly required no deliberation at all.

Perhaps the most striking case of acting without deliberating is that of deliberation itself. Imagine that I deliberate as to which book to assign my introductory class. As likely as not, my deliberation does not spring from deliberation: one moment I was thinking about something else, and the next moment I was wondering what book I should assign to my class. If we were to assume that actions are rational only if they are the result of deliberation, deliberating about my textbooks would not have been a rational act. It is, though: it is a sign of my (relative) rationality that I begin to deliberate about next semester's textbooks just about now. Furthermore, the thought that deliberating, in order to be a rational action, would have to be the result of deliberation seems to threaten an infinite regress: before deliberating about my textbooks, I would have had to deliberate about deliberating about my textbooks, and before that deliberate about deliberating about deliberating, and so forth, in order for all these intellectual acts to prove to be rational.

In a similar vein, it can be pointed out that the course of my deliberation about my textbooks depends on non-deliberative inferences. When I ask myself "Which books should I assign?" it is not an accident that the initial list of books that occur to me as candidates does not include *What Does It All Mean?* or *Being and Time* but does include *Philosophical Ethics* and *Knowledge and the Flow of Information*. From prior knowledge of students at my institution, I have concluded without deliberation that *What Does It All Mean?* would appear deceptively easy to my challenge-hungry students, who would as a result not study it hard enough, and that *Being and Time* would appear, and actually be, too difficult for all my students. Thus, neither book appears on my list, though either could have appeared on it if I were teaching different students. When I turn to trying to decide between the books on my list, I quickly turn to wondering whether *Knowledge and the Flow of Information* is too difficult or not: I do not waste much time wondering if *Philosophical Ethics* is too difficult. If you were to interrupt my reflection by asking why I do not doubt the accessibility of *Philosophical Ethics*, I might tell you in reply that *Philosophical Ethics* is obviously accessible to my university's students, but if you were not to ask me this question, the thought would never have consciously occurred to me. Thus, every step that I take in deliberation is informed in a non-deliberative way by beliefs and desires that do not participate in it.

That every step in deliberation, including the first step, is thus informed by our prior knowledge in a non-deliberative way is also the conclusion of empirical study. In his (1994) book *Descartes' Error*, Antonio Damasio describes the predicament of patients who have lost the ability to have emotional feelings as a result of brain injury, while their intellects have remained intact. If one believes in the traditional dichotomy between Reason and Appetite, one will expect that these "cold-blooded" people would be hyper-rational. However, these people seem to be utter failures exactly in the realm of practical reasoning—or, as the author puts it, in choosing the best means to reach their aims. In attempting to keep a job, make a good business deal, or win a card game, the people studied by Damasio consistently make very bad decisions. Why are the non-feelers bad at practical rationality? Consider again my deliberation involving textbooks. My deliberation focuses on *Knowledge and the Flow of Information* because the thought of assigning it invokes a feeling of uneasiness or worry. It does not focus on *Philosophical Ethics* because assigning the latter "feels right." I never considered *Being and Time* because the idea would make me laugh. Thus, even my calm, academic deliberation seems to be guided by subtle emotional cues—cues that I hardly notice. We should not pretend that for the deliberation to proceed, I have to tell myself "Ok, I feel uneasy about this book, maybe that's a reason to reconsider it," the way a master might wonder why his dog is barking. This scenario is possible, but another scenario is at least as likely, in which I take no such reflective step: I simply proceed from coming up with a list of possible books to thinking further about one book, as opposed to the others, without taking any time to introspect about my feelings. My uneasiness about *Knowledge and the Flow of Information* simply is part of my process of reasoning—the part in which my previous experience with students, books, and so forth, weighs in to guide my decision. Brain-damaged non-feelers, despite an unharmed ability to deliberate and reflect, seem to make bad decisions because they are denied such feeling-based access to their own background knowledge in making those decisions. Thus, despite being able to deliberate, they end up doing things that no rational person would have done—the same way that no rational person would have assigned *Being and Time* to my students in Introduction to Philosophy. The rational person, and not the brain-damaged person, would *feel amused* at the thought and give it no further attention.[6]

---

[6] Similar results are discussed by Churchland (1996).

Two things, then, appear to be true. First, if we were to assume that only actions that are the result of deliberation are rational, we would discover that it is never rational for an agent to deliberate, as the act of deliberation must, at some point, spring from something other than deliberation. Second, no action and no belief is purely the result of deliberation. Assigning *Philosophical Ethics* to my students is the result of deliberation, but it is also the result of many beliefs and inferences that formed no part of my deliberation.

Christopher Hookway (2000) also notices that rational people differ from less rational people when it comes to the sort of things that occur to them before or during deliberation, describing phenomena not unlike the ones described above. However, he attributes the fact to "habit": we who are more practiced at deliberation are habituated to starting and finishing deliberation at appropriate times, after drawing upon appropriate considerations. And if Hookway is right, then there is some reason to think that the sorts of unthinkingly skilled actions I have described are all done out of complex habits, and hence are not really reason-responsive after all. But where would Hookway's hypothesized habits of deliberation come from? It is psychologically unlikely that we spend childhood deliberating on the right way to deliberate, practicing deliberating until we start from the right point, bringing to mind and ignoring the right things. Children are, if anything, *less* reflective than adults, and children who are beginning to deliberate are not intensely self-conscious deliberating engines, taking all of their deliberative steps explicitly. A seven-year-old boy wondering whether he will get caught taking a cookie does not ask himself whether, in asking the question, he has taken disobedience too lightly, does not consider whether parental reactions are really the only ones worth considering (might there be reputational effects on peers or siblings?), and so on. Deliberating is *never* a highly explicit activity that becomes routinized out of habit. It *does* become more skilled as we grow older, but not because we have automated procedures that once were explicit. Rather, things like gathering data by experience and trial and error are responsible for our increases in skill in deliberation, responsible without in any way implicating a reason-unresponsive mechanism. It seems perfectly good English to say that I have improved my mental *habits*, but the use of the word 'habit' must not obscure the fact that what is learned is not a mere automation process, but rather a set of highly sophisticated, information-sensitive, reason-responsive skills.

Let us now switch from deliberation itself to other forms of apparent rationality without deliberation. If one is used to thinking of acting for reasons as always involving deliberation, it is easy to think that everything else that looks like acting for reasons is sheer habit. Thus, one might think that though a good athlete is reason-responsive while in the field, he is only derivatively so, because, after being properly trained and habituated, he made a rational decision to "trust his instincts," instincts that are not directly reason-responsive. But first of all, there are cases of fast action in which such a story is empirically implausible—consider again the person who is a witty conversationalist, who obviously responds to reason when she talks but whose actions are unlikely to be the result of any rote learning, at any point. Second, consider the fact that even if, in a given situation, the athlete or the conversationalist did somehow make a conscious decision to follow her instincts—suppose the conversationalist, on her way to a job interview, decides to "just be herself" —she can still be criticized as irrational if she does something stupid, even if that does not detract from the rationality of her initial decision to follow her so-called instincts. If, subliminally affected by the fact that one of the interviewers' face reminds her of her cruel uncle, the conversationalist, for just one moment, speaks with a defensiveness that she would usually avoid; she acts irrationally. If we truly believed that once she makes a decision to trust her instincts, the rest of her behavior is merely some type of mechanism that the decision activated like a reflex hammer, we would not fault her if her reflex, by some quirk, failed to point her the right way just once, but this is not our response to such cases.

It is important to see that even if one's actions can be reasonably explained by acquired habit—especially a complex habit, the kind of 'habit' that explains the actions of athletes, witty conversationalists, and deliberators—it is a mistake to assume that that just because the word *habit* applies, the "habitual" actions are not reason-responsive. These habits are not like reflexes, nor like the instincts of simple animals, nor are they "automatic" in any deeper sense than that they do not require reflection. Consider some differences between habit and reflex. A reflex, of the sort tested with a reflex hammer, is indifferent to the beliefs and the desires of the person in whose body the reflex has been triggered. On the other hand, while driving to work is often governed by something that can be rightly called habit, it is not as if you have hit a reflex hammer when you entered the car and then for the rest of the way ceased to be an active agent. Your actions, unlike knee jerks, are still sensitive to such things as your desire to stay alive or your belief that there is a truck on your left, and if a confusing situation occurs, deliberation comes into play as if on cue.

In fact, it is important to see that complex forms of habituation can be something that *enable* a person to respond to reasons—just as sophisticated

contemporary psychotropic medication can enable a person, in some respects, to be more rational. By acting rationally, again, I mean more than
doing what the rational person would do or what you would do if you were
rational, but rather acting *for* good reasons. Consider again the somewhat
grim example of responding to the threat of machine-gun fire. The best
response to being machine gunned, generally, is to throw oneself flat on
the ground (giving one a less vulnerable profile). But even people who
know this fact are generally inclined to act irrationally if machine gunned
and run away (thus remaining highly exposed). After extended habituation,
however, people are capable of responding the right way (this is a typical
part of soldierly training). Now imagine a person who does not need to be
habituated. Before knowing what the right response is, he too would have
fled a machine-gun attack, but having acquired the intellectual knowledge
about appropriate responses, is now disposed to unthinkingly act the right
way in this perilous situation. Even without having made a conscious decision to act on his unthinking inclinations, such a person is disposed to act
rationally: so much seems obvious. But the person who reaches this state
by habituation is like the person who reaches a state of rationality by taking
lithium instead of by being born sane. Under fire, there is no need to think
that his state of mind is any different from that of the person who was lucky
enough not to have needed the training. The latter has been trained not
only out of doing the wrong thing, but into being, with respect to certain
situations, more properly reason responsive and rational. It is true that
complex habits do not guarantee that one acts rationally, but as I have
mentioned earlier, neither does deliberation.

Last but not least, every view that maintains that somehow every action
that seems rational and non-deliberate somehow owes its rationality to a
prior deliberation needs to account for the facts (1) that human beings start
their lives as small children unable to deliberate and then develop the ability to deliberate—not the other way round; and (2) that the human race
evolved from nondeliberating animals. These facts alone put a burden of
proof on anyone who wants to argue that deliberation came first and habits
of deliberation came second.

Of the Difference between Epilepsy and Apoplexy

Let us return to the matter at hand. The view that without contracausal
freedom, we would be like robots seemed to require that one deny the

efficacy of mental content, but holding this view forces philosophers working primarily on free will to engage with materialist philosophers of mind working on content efficacy, an engagement not likely to favor the theorists of free will. Romantic incompatibilists might counter with a modified version of the view, claiming that without contracausal freedom, we would not be like robots but we would be like, say, mice: creatures whose mental lives include some content efficacy, but no responsiveness to reasons. Let us explore for a moment the difference, in human lives, between what appears to be 'robot causation', 'content-efficacious causation' and 'reason responsiveness'.

Consider the following three scenarios:

1. Julius calls me an idiot, raising his voice in the process. As a result, my ears hurt.
2. Julius calls me an idiot, raising his voice in the process. Because of a troubled upbringing and Julius's resemblance to my father, I feel diminished and inferior.
3. Julius calls me an idiot, raising his voice in the process. As a result I conclude that Julius must be having a very hard day today.

The second scenario, unlike the first, involves content efficacy. The fact that I hear a cry of "Idiot!" instead of a cry of "I love you!" certainly influences my reaction, which it does not in the first scenario. Yet I respond to the content of Julius's remark because he is a father figure, not because I think he is likely to be right in his judgment of me. This is not true reason responsiveness. Reason responsiveness comes in the third scenario. Whatever happens between my hearing Julius's cry and my believing that he is having a hard day involves an inference. Consciously or otherwise, something has taken place that must be counted as reasoning.

Or consider the following, somewhat different three scenarios:

1. Nicola is in a sad mood. This is the result of light deprivation; she has been exposed to an arctic winter.
2. Nicola is in a sad mood. This is the result of the effect of being exposed to surroundings that vaguely resemble the scene of a sad love affair from her past.
3. Nicola is in a sad mood. This is because, judging by the six o'clock news, the world is still full of sexism.

While it might be strange to think of moods as responding to reasons, Nicola's reaction to the six o'clock news seems to require the ability to respond to reasons. It even makes sense to say that the state of sexism in the world is a *good* reason to be sad. On the other hand, the fact that one is surrounded by sights and sounds that resemble those that surrounded a bad experience is not a *reason* to be sad. Still, there is content efficacy in this scenario that does not exist in the first. One might wish to call the second scenario 'psychological', and the first one 'merely chemical', or perhaps to speak of an 'irrational' reaction as opposed to an 'arational' one.

Last but not least, consider these three situations, inspired by Donald Davidson's famous discussion of acting for reasons (1980):

1. Emma drops a copy of *Being and Time* on George's head because she is having a grand mal seizure.
2. Emma drops a copy of *Being and Time* on George's head because she is so angry at him that her hand shakes and the book slips from her grasp.
3. Emma throws a copy of *Being and Time* at George because she is angry at him.

In the third situation, Emma throws the book in response to a practical reason. Emma is acting even if she is not deliberating while throwing the book, and even if, while she is doing it, she is wondering if she's out of her mind or thinking "I'll regret it later." But in the second case, I take it that dropping the book is not an action: it is not done in order to achieve anything. Still, the second case does involve content efficacy. The contents of thoughts about George cause anger, and this anger, which causes the shaking, presumably would not be there if the thought was "I like frogs" instead. Shaking at the thought of an outrage and shaking because one is having an epileptic fit are different things, even though in both cases, one does not shake "for a reason" and one does not perform an action. Hence there is a difference between the second case and the first.

I have argued that the romantic incompatibilist cannot make the robot claim without denying content efficacy. In response, the romantic incompatibilist might offer the following modified view: without denying content efficacy, it can still be true that human beings who are 'caused' are incapable of *responding to reasons*—both epistemic and practical. In a caused world, the proposal goes, we can still be sad, afraid, pleased, or attracted—things that, admittedly, robots cannot be. However, our mental repertory would be limited by an inability to act, believe, or feel for a reason. We can have fits of anger, not only epileptic fits, but we cannot be angry for a reason, or *act* out of anger-related reasons. And this is an important matter, because paradigmatic cases of romantic necessity involve responsiveness to reasons. Thus, the romantic incompatibilist can hang on to his previous claims— that love, art, and the like lose their meaning in a deterministic world—

without taking on the robot view. All he needs to say is that determinism precludes reason responsiveness—or at the very least, "enough" reason responsiveness to allow for meaningful romantic necessity.

For example, the person who "cannot tell a lie" is only impressive if, one way or another, he is responding to "the right" reasons not to lie: he is not impressive if he is only prevented from lying by aversion created by the hidden memory of his parents' punishment. For my love of you to be ultimately valuable, it ought to be the case that it is partially a reflection of reason-responsiveness: I am able to understand your great virtues and staggering intellect, or to feel a compassionate "connection" to twists of your psyche that are similar to mine (which requires some understanding of them, however implicit). There is not much value in my love if it is merely something akin to an animal's tendency to feel some sweet sensation at the sight of creatures with large eyes or a three-year-old's attraction to soft things. Luther's motivation to do no other, if it is to be meaningful, should be based on a rather complex system of beliefs and motivations that is surely impossible without the ability to respond to reasons. While it might be quite hard to pin down the aesthetic reasons to which a writer or a painter might be responding, we still imagine her as driven by some complex artistic truth or wish to express an inner vision. And of course, the person whose mind is "seized" by a new mathematical truth or who "cannot" believe in astrology due to her intelligence is responding to her epistemic reasons (to the evidence available to her). Without reason responsiveness, mental events can still cause each other in a way that is not content-free, but there is nothing for the romantic compatibilist in what is left. Our beliefs and moods need not be content-free robot-like states, if determinism is true, but they would also be far from being meaningful in the more robust sense in which incompatibilists fear that our lives would lose their meanings.

I suspect that Susan Wolf's nightmare scenario below is similar to what we can imagine the world to be if we have no reason responsiveness or if we have only limited capacity to respond to reasons: "We would still be able to form some sorts of associations that could be described as friendship and love. One person could find another amusing or useful. One could notice that the presence of a certain person was, like the sound of a favorite song, particularly soothing or invigorating. . . . [A]ttachments of considerable strength can develop on such limited bases. People do, after all, form strong attachments to their cars, their pianos, not to mention their pets" (Wolf 1993a, 166).

If we grant the existence of content efficacy, why should we believe that there is no reason responsiveness in a causally determined world? If it is already agreed that we are not robots, why stop at the "lower animals" level? I suspect that given the existence of content efficacy, there can be many possible theories of reason-responsiveness that would be compatible with a causally determined world, but let me discuss the particular kind of view that I wish to offer.

Absolute Reasons and Rationalizing Reasons

In *Swimming to Antarctica* Lynn Cox tells us that when she was a girl, her swimming coach—a world-class one—noticed that unlike her fellow swimming students, she tended to become more energetic after a long workout than before the workout, as if she was just then getting into gear. He also noticed that she was a bit restless and listless, despite excellent performance, as if the pool was too small for her. That discovery led him to infer that Cox had the makings of an excellent long-distance swimmer, the sort that swims the English Channel. He suggested to her that she take up long-distance swimming (a sport she did not know much about and that people of her tender age rarely excelled at). The rest, as they say, is history: Cox was launched into a rewarding career as the best long-distance swimmer of her time, and gained fame when she became the first person to swim across the Bering Strait.

When the coach approached Cox, it is natural to say that he sensed that Cox had *good reasons* to try long-distance swimming. It is easy to imagine the reasons: Cox wanted very deeply to become a high-achieving athlete, had the necessary devotion, and also the physical and mental tendencies to become a high-achieving endurance swimmer. Also, her frustration suggested that she would like long-distance swimming better than the ordinary kind: she seemed, whether she knew it or not, to have a craving for wider spaces. If Cox were to ask the coach, "What reason do I have to take up long-distance swimming?" he could point out the above reasons. If his views on reasons were loftier, he could have offered her some others. Perhaps, for example, the coach believed that the very fact that one has a special talent was by itself a reason to develop the talent, regardless of the talented person's desires. If this were true, the reason Cox had a reason to take up long-distance swimming was simply her talent.

As I said, it is not unnatural to say that Cox always had reasons—including reasons that are rooted in her own desires—to take up long-distance swimming, but she did not know about these reasons until the coach pointed them out. The coach did not create her reasons, but revealed to her that she had them all along. On the other hand, there is a perfectly good sense in which Cox did not have a reason to take up long-distance swimming until her coach informed her that the sport existed and that she showed the signs of talent for it. I am not simply saying that without the coach's suggestion, nothing would have *motivated* Cox to take up long-distance swimming, but I am suggesting that there is a sense in which she also has no reason to do so. This sense is illustrated by the following intuitive judgments:

1. Before hearing the coach's view, the fact that Cox never tried long-distance swimming does not imply that anything was wrong with her as a rational or reasonable agent. She is ignorant of certain facts about long-distance swimming and the ways one can spot an aptitude for it, but there is nothing wrong with her reasoning. On the other hand, after she heard the coach's judgment, if she still fails to take up long-distance swimming, it is something that she has, in a sense, to account for: absent weightier reasons to the contrary, she would be *irrational* not to give it a try.

2. If Cox took up long-distance swimming before hearing the coach's view, or without in some other way knowing of her talent, her decision would seem rash or even irrational. Why, after all, would she aim at such a crazy goal as swimming the English Channel? And at age fifteen? Absent some special story, Cox would seem like a crazy teenager who accidentally ended up doing something that she had a reason to do.

Let us say that before hearing her coach, Cox did not have a *rationalizing reason* to take up long-distance swimming, a reason that would make it *reasonable* for her to take up swimming. This is true despite the fact that she had what might be called an *absolute* reason. Having an absolute reason does not imply anything about one's rationality or reasonableness, while having a rationalizing reason does (see Davidson 1980). Note that by 'rationalizing' I do not just mean 'explanatory' or 'capable of making understandable'. After all, there are cases in which it is quite understandable that someone acts irrationally (as in "It's understandable that so soon after the death of her husband, she was not thinking straight"). Nor is a rationalizing reason the same as a motivating reason in the sense described by Michael Smith (1994). Absent better reasons to disobey her coach, if Cox is motivated by a rationalizing reason, it not only makes her action understandable but also rational, and if she fails to be motivated by a rationalizing reason, it makes her behavior irrational, even if it has a good explanation (say, adolescent resistance to the authoritative coach). To borrow a famous example from Bernard Williams (1981, 102), we can say that if I want to drink gin, I have an absolute reason to drink the gin in the glass before me even if, in fact, I believe it to be something else, but I do not have a *rationalizing* reason to drink it unless I do take it to be gin. If I think—however falsely—that the glass is full of gasoline, it would be quite irrational of me to drink something I take to be gasoline. If it happened to be gin I would be lucky, like the rash person who mistakenly thinks that swallowing a lot of aspirin is a good suicide method, and so is spared from rashly committing suicide. I am not, however, any less crazy. If the liquid is in fact gin, but I believe it to be gasoline, my rationalizing reasons and my absolute reasons point in different directions. A similar distinction to mine has been proposed by Mele (2003, 79).

It is also important to note that the distinction between rationalizing and absolute reasons is not the familiar distinction between internal and external reasons. We could think of Cox's absolute reasons as internal—as grounded in the various desires she has that would be satisfied by taking up long-distance swimming—or we might think that she has absolute reasons whatever her desires are: for example, we might think that every talented person has a reason to develop her talent. In neither case do her absolute reasons by themselves give her rationalizing reasons. If Cox's absolute reasons are desire-independent and grounded only in the fact of her talent, it is still true that if Cox did not know of her talent, whether explicitly and reflectively or otherwise, she would have no rationalizing reason to develop it. Similarly, if Cox's absolute reasons depend on her desires, it would still be true that, in ignorance of those reasons, Cox would have no rationalizing reason to develop her talents.

The Cox example involves practical reasons. It is possible, albeit less natural, to make a similar distinction when it comes to epistemic reasons. There have always been reasons to believe that the earth is round, but it might be that very long ago, no one had rationalizing reasons to believe that the earth is round. "Are there reasons to believe that the universe is expanding?" is not the same question as "Do I have reasons to believe that the universe is expanding?" If I ask the first question, you are likely to answer "yes," but the answer to the second question is, in some cases, "With your lack of background knowledge, I can't see what reasons you have to believe that the universe is expanding. But if you listen to me a little bit, I'll *give* you some reasons."

When a philosopher makes such a claim as "only desires provide us with reasons to act," it is important to note whether the philosopher saying that all *absolute* reasons to act are provided by desires or that all *rationalizing* reasons to act are provided by desire. The first claim seems false: not only do some absolute reasons have nothing to do with desires; they often have nothing to do with mental states of any kind. My reasons to give money to the Lance Armstrong Foundation stem from the state of the fight against cancer, not my mental states. My reasons to believe that tapirs are mammals stem from the fact that they are warm-blooded and furry, not my mental states. This, however, does not rule out the possibility that the second claim—that all *rationalizing* reasons depend on desires—is true.[7] Consider, by analogy, reasons to believe. If you ask me why I believe my student, Ms. D'Acosta, is probably from Goa, I would provide you with what I regard to be reasons for thus believing: "She looks Indian but her name sounds Portuguese. This is quite rare in people who are not from Goa." This is a list of putative absolute reasons, and it is a list of facts about my student and about Goa—nowhere in the list need there be anything about me, or the set of beliefs that I, Nomy, happen to have, nor need there be any reference to beliefs or believing at all. The word "belief" need appear nowhere in my reflection about my student, because what I am trying to find for myself and inform you about are absolute reasons for believing that the student is from Goa. But *rationalizing* reasons to believe are always provided by other beliefs. If I knew nothing about Goans and if, nonetheless, knowing my student only by face and name, I develop the belief "she must be from Goa," I would be irrational or arational: I would be developing a strong conviction for *no reason at all*, and one would be right to suspect that something had gone wrong with my brain.

   Just as many of our absolute reasons to believe have nothing to do with our beliefs, it is relatively easy to show that our *absolute* reasons for actions often have nothing to with our desires. Imagine that Martha hates herself and thinks that her desires are unimportant. She neglects her own well-being and does not seem to care whether or not she remains alive. Fortunately for many of us, it is quite untrue that "you have to love yourself before you can love anybody," and so Martha, despite hating herself, loves someone else—let's call her Nicola. While unwilling to do anything for her own well-being, Martha is ready to do a lot to make Nicola happy— we can even imagine that when Martha contemplates suicide, she is stopped only by the thought that her existence might be of help to Nicola. Imagine that Martha does something good for Nicola—say, sends her some chocolate. Martha reasons from the premise "Nicola could use some cheering

---

[7] A similar point is made by Petit and Smith (1990).

up." She is not thinking anything as selfish or self-important as "I, Martha, desire Nicola's happiness, and because I have this desire, I should send her some chocolate." That Nicola could use cheering up sounds like a perfectly good absolute reason to send Nicola chocolate, and it has nothing to do with Martha's desires, or anyone else's. To merely point this out, however, is not yet to eliminate the possibility that if she had a different set of desires and concerns—if she did not, say, care intrinsically about Nicola's happiness—Martha would have no *rationalizing* reasons to send her some chocolate, just as, if I did not have certain background beliefs, my student's name and face would not have been a rationalizing reason for me to conclude that she is from Goa. Perhaps if Martha did not have certain background desires, Nicola's need for cheering up would not have been a rationalizing reason for her to send her chocolates.

The question of whether or not one can have rationalizing reasons to do something without some desires, known or unknown to one, that would be satisfied by doing it cannot be resolved simply by pointing out that we do not always consider our desires when we deliberate. Just because I do something for Rachel's sake doesn't mean that I would have a rationalizing reason to do it if I did not love her. While the distinction between rationalizing and absolute reasons makes it harder to make a popular objection to the internal reasons view, it does not by itself provide an argument against the existence of external reasons. It might still be possible, for example, to show that certain beliefs are connected to certain desires such that if only one understands certain facts (say, the objective value of another person), then one would be irrational in some way not to have the desire.

The ground has now been prepared for sketching an account of reason-responsiveness. If mental states typically display content efficacy, it is hard to see why it would not be possible for mental states to cause one another by virtue of particular properties of their content. For example, the experience of reading a story distresses me by virtue of the plot's sadness or by virtue of the story's artistic inferiority. My belief "Kari is a Brown student" and my belief "All Brown students are smart" can produce other beliefs in me by virtue of their contents—and also by virtue of special features of their contents. One feature of their content is the fact that there is a certain logical relation between them that makes "Kari is smart" a good thing to infer. To the extent that my beliefs "Kari is a Brown student" and "All Brown students are smart" produce the belief that Kari is smart *by virtue of* that "rationalizing relationship" between them—by virtue of their contents being the good premises for a valid argument in favor of the proposition "Kari is smart"—to that extent, I suggest, my belief that Kari is smart develops for a reason, is a result of my reason-responsive nature. Suppose that I believe that all Brown students are smart and that Kari is a Brown student. Together, these beliefs provide a rationalizing reason for me to believe that Kari is smart. However, in order to say that I believe that Kari is smart *for* this reason, it has to be true that I believe that Kari is smart because, consciously or otherwise, I inferred it from "Kari is a Brown student" and "Brown students are smart." To say that the belief is the result of my inference is to say not simply that the belief "Kari is smart" was caused by the other two beliefs, nor simply to say that the belief "Kari is smart" was caused by the two beliefs by virtue of their content, but to say that it was caused by the content of the two beliefs by virtue of a certain logical relation that exists between the contents of the beliefs. One might justly wonder what it means for one thing to cause another by virtue of something, but this question does not point to a particular problem with beliefs and rationalizing relationships: one might equally wonder what it means for a rock to break a window by virtue of its weight, and I only presuppose that whatever sensible answer can be given to the latter question can also be given to the former.

Something similar can be said about acting for a reason. If the content of a group of mental states—under the most common story these would be beliefs and desires, but they do not have to be—adds up to compelling reasons to do something, and these mental states motivate me to do it by virtue of the very feature that makes them good reasons, good premises in a practical inference—then I have responded to a reason. Suppose, for example, that Emma's desire to hurt George and her belief that she would hurt George by dropping a copy of *Being and Time* on his head give her a reason to drop a copy of *Being and Time* on George's head while George is sitting. Suppose that Emma in fact drops a copy of *Being and Time* on George's head while George is sitting. According to Davidson (1980) Emma drops the book for a reason if her dropping the book is the result of the desire to hurt George and her belief that dropping the book will hurt George: but by way of objection to Davidson it has been pointed out that this is not always true (e.g., Sehon 1997; Wilson 1997). For example, if the desire and the belief make her nervous, and as a result her copy of *Being and Time* falls on George's head, it seems that Emma did not drop the book on George's head for a reason. For Emma to drop the book on George's head *in order* to hurt him, it has to be true not only that the relevant belief and desire caused her to drop the book (Davidson's condition), but also that the belief and the desire caused her to drop the book *by virtue of the thing that makes them a rationalizing reason for her to do so.* That is, not by other features they have, and not even by other features of their content, such as their unnerving nature, but by virtue of the fact that their contents makes them good premises for a practical inference that points toward dropping the book on George's head. The "by virtue" is essential here, while the appeal to the belief-desire model of reasons could, in principle, be replaced by appeal to some other view of practical inference. The important thing is that the relevant mental states cause the dropping of the book by virtue of the very logical relations that make them the premises of a valid practical inference toward dropping the book.

I do not deny that my account, too, is vulnerable to objections from deviant causal chains: it is not clear exactly what it means for something to cause something "by virtue" of a particular fact about it. But again, this problem is not particular to actions or to cases involving mental states: it is equally hard to explain what it means for a rock to break a window by virtue of its size and weight. For one account of how such causation can go, see Mele's *Motivation and Agency* (2004).

This is where one might confront me with a different sort of problem that plagued Davidson's view. It seems as if every action, in order to be an action at all, has to be for a reason. There are cases in which we act—and thus, act for reasons—and cases in which we do not act at all, as happens in seizures and shudders. How does one explain a case in which a person acts—and yet acts *irrationally?* I could add a further question here: how does one explain the many shades of gray between acting rationally and acting mildly irrationally and being utterly insane?

Let me start by pointing out one important difference between my view and Davidson's. Davidson, for many theoretical reasons, is committed to the view that the best overall explanation for a person's behavior is the most rationalizing explanation—the explanation that makes it appear most rational (see, e.g., Davidson 1980). While I take it that an action, in order to be an action, has to be done for a reason, nothing about my view commits me to the claim that the best overall explanation of a person's behavior is the most rationalizing explanation. Unlike Davidson, I do not even believe that we usually assume, by default, that the person we are trying to understand is rational. Judging by how surprised we can be when someone acts with unusual rationality, there is at least one sense in which it is not necessarily so. In disbelief, we ask such things as "You mean you weren't a little jealous"? "You mean you weren't tempted, at least a bit?" We say, "So John really did have good reason to buy that red car. We all assumed that it was a midlife crisis thing." We do, to be sure, make default assumptions about people we try to understand, but these assumptions vary. Often, our default assumption when trying to understand a person is that the person we are trying to understand is *similar to us*. Naturally, a person who is very rational will tend to assume that other people are rational as well, but if we take ourselves to suffer from some irrationality, we might be inclined to assume by default that other people also share that irrationality. For example, a person who is irrationally fearful will tend to attribute your abandonment of a project to irrational fear before even considering another explanation, and a person who is vain will be likely to assume by default that your liking for playing chess at coffee shops or your use of long words is motivated by vanity. At other times, we assume that the person we are trying to understand might not be like us, but is *similar to what we take to be an ordinary person*—a possessor of common sense, but also common human irrationalities. We are surprised, for example, to see a parent who does not suffer from the occasional irrational worry about her offspring, an American woman who does not have some irrational attitudes toward her weight, a student who never procrastinates her work, or anyone at all who is not susceptible to flattery or sensual temptations (if we use this assumption, we are also surprised, of course, by someone who is more irrational than average: we might, for example, refuse to believe that a depressed person is depressed for no reason at all). Some people hold more idiosyncratic default assumptions. For example, a person might hold that *to understand is to forgive*, which means that when she tries to explain the behavior of fellow human beings, she will reach for the explanation that makes their actions most morally excusable—which is just as likely to be an "irrationalizing" explanation as a rationalizing one, as when a person assumes that a murderer must have been temporarily insane when he committed his crime. Or a person might hold the opposite assumption, *people are mean bastards until proven otherwise*—thus being prone to misinterpreting the behavior of those who mean well. And so on.

On my view, human beings being what they are, the best overall explanation of a piece of human behavior or belief will often be an explanation that presents it as a mixture of the reason-responsive, the merely-content-responsive, and the robot-like—and woven fine, too. For a movement to be an action, all that needs to be true is that the immediate cause of the movement be of the reason-responsive kind—a rationalizing belief desire pair: but the immediate cause is just a part of the story. Events, including actions and mental events, are not the effects of a single "immediate" cause but of a general "causal circumstance" —for example, the cigarette catching fire is not just the effect of your operating the lighter but also of the fact that there is oxygen in the room and many other facts as well. The sort of explanations that we seek in real life or in psychologically informed detective stories generally involve not only the immediate belief-desire pair that led to the action but other parts of the causal circumstance as well. If you wonder why the chicken crossed the road, and learn that it wanted to get to the other side and believed crossing the road would achieve this, you know the immediate cause and reason for the crossing, but not the whole story. If the chicken's behavior baffles you, and you decide it requires an explanation, you will ask more and more questions about the circumstance in the chicken's brain until things start to make sense. Admittedly, crossing a road is rarely a very baffling action (though it can be a whimsical one), and so we don't often find ourselves trying to explain such actions. But imagine one such scenario, and the way in which an explanation-seeking conversation might proceed:

> **You**: Why did Chicken cross the road?
> **Me**: Because he thought he saw Duck standing there by the gas station. He wanted to say "hi."
> **You**: But Chicken knows she is out of town.
> **Me**: He's in love with Duck. You know how he is when he's obsessed.
> **You**: And he really thought she would be pleased, seeing him cross the road after her in the middle of the night? She would have freaked out.
> **Me**: Oh, he must have been a little drunk, too.
> **You**: Yes, that sounds like him.

This conversation demonstrates a few things. First, as the original joke shows, when we seek an explanation for someone's behavior, we often ask for a lot more than the belief/desire pair that ultimately caused the action. It might take a bit of a tour through a person's mind before even a moderately baffling action stops being baffling. Often, if we are trying to understand another person's truly baffling action, the tour is much longer than in my example, whether at the end we regard the person as acting rationally or not. Second, what appears to be the most plausible explanation for the behavior of the agent is not an explanation that makes him seem very rational. Nor is it necessarily the most rationalizing explanation you can find. If one was trying hard to look for the most rationalizing explanation for our chicken's behavior, one would not stop so early at such explanations as "he was drunk" or "love turned his head." But in general, one does not look for the most rationalizing explanation, but simply for what seemed to be the likeliest and most economical explanation, given the evidence (such as the agent's past record of being occasionally drunk). Third, the explanation happens to involve robot causation (drunkenness), some reason responsiveness (an active belief/desire pair), and some content causation that isn't reason-responsiveness (wishful thinking leading to misidentification). The three kinds of causation are, again, woven fine, and one often needs to mention processes of more than one kind in order to come up with an explanation.

Note another feature of the view sketched here that makes it easier for it to deal with irrational action: the category of content-responsiveness that is not reason-responsiveness. For Davidson, there seem to be two ways in which mental events can cause things: as reasons or qua mere brain states. This leaves such phenomena as wishful thinking in need of explanation, because while the fact that I wish there were no school today is certainly no reason to believe that it is in fact the case, it is also not some kind of freak neural accident that the mental state known as 'wanting it to be the case that there is no school today' happened to cause in me the belief that there is no school today, and not, for example, the belief that pigs have wings. On my view, however, there is no such prima facie difficulty, because wishful thinking can simply be one type of case in which we are caused to believe in a way in which content is efficacious but reason responsiveness does not occur. Other cases include seeing yourself as ugly because you hate yourself or seeing your uncle as big because you fear him. In similar ways, content-efficacy without reason responsiveness also allows us to explain, without resorting to Freudian divisions in the mind, how things such as fear or laziness can derail what would have been rational actions. Mental states can cause other mental states in ways that involve their contents but no rationalizing relationships, and so, for example, an embarrassing memory of the last time the secretary laughed at me (very long ago, she meant well, and she has forgotten it anyway) might undermine my motivation to go to her office. It might undermine it so badly that many mental states which could potentially have moved me, by virtue of rationalizing relationships, to go to her office now fail to do so, and I stay home irrationally.

Another example: I hear that Joseph slapped his child. The fact baffles me, as Joseph isn't known to do such things. So I ask for an explanation. "Why did he hit his child?" I ask. The explanation I get is this: Well, Joseph wanted his child to stop nagging, so he hit him so it would stop. Now, this usually would not have been enough to motivate him, since he cares about his child and is a competent parent, but he was very, very angry at George W. Bush that day, and his boss yelled at him, and his team lost, and then there's this situation with his brother in the hospital, so the nagging made him feel stretched to the limit. He would have been able to prevent himself from hitting the child anyway, but one must remember that he hadn't slept for two days, and that interferes with your self-control.

This fairly ordinary explanation is a hybrid mix of reason-responsiveness, unreasoned content-responsiveness, and robotic, non-content causation. The reason responsiveness comes in because the man hit his child *in order* to make the child stop nagging, because he wanted to make the child stop nagging and believed that hitting would achieve that effect. The unreasoned content-responsiveness comes in because the man would never have minded the nagging so much if he were not angry already. Joseph's anger at his boss and/or George W. Bush is not a reason to be upset at his child's nagging, but it is a state the content of which is relevant for its effect on Joseph, since being angry involves perceiving oneself as being attacked, and hitting is a relevant response to an attack. The "hardware" causation comes in because even with the other factors in place, Joseph would have managed to prevent himself from actually hitting the child if it were not for the completely atavistic effects of the sleep deprivation. And this fairly ordinary explanation is compatible both with our holding that Joseph's hitting the child is an action and with our holding that, all in all, he was acting irrationally in hitting the child. Joseph's hitting the child is an action—he did it because of a belief and a desire and by virtue of the rationalizing relationship between them. However, he might still, all in all, be acting irrationally because it might be that Joseph has, given his desires, beliefs, and the like, overwhelming rationalizing reasons to refrain from hitting the child, and he failed to respond to them. Why? Perhaps his anger and his sleep deprivation prevented him from doing so.

I said that Joseph's action is overall irrational because it now seems that most human behavior has some "method" to it and some "madness" to it (and, in modern parlance, some chemistry involved too). On balance, there is more madness in Joseph's hitting the child than method. The same action (or, for that matter, the same belief) can have in it different mixes of madness and method, reasonability and unreasonableness. I have been told by a psychiatrist that "Hemingway, when he was manic, thought he was a great writer." This sentence is funny, and one's natural reaction is to say, "And what was he really, chopped liver?" How irrational was Hemingway when he developed this belief? It is hard to tell. One scenario is that Hemingway was only mildly manic, and he believed that he was a great writer for the same good reasons for which we regard him as such, although he was also dreadfully excited, sleepless about it, unable to contain his glory, and perhaps felt irrationally invincible because of it. Another scenario is that Hemingway was very, very manic. He would have believed that he was a great writer even if the evidence suggested otherwise, even if he were a composer of badly scanned limericks, but it just happened to be the case, by some devilish irony, that his delusion coincided with the truth. In similar ways, it can be hard to tell, from the outside, how much a person's action is the result of reasons and to what extent it is not so. Did your colleague support the job candidate for the good reasons he had (say, her merits) or was he irrationally and probably unconsciously swayed by something else (the fact that both he and the candidate own elkhounds, which contributes to a sense of friendly familiarity)? We can imagine a scenario in which it is true that if the candidate did not own a dog, your colleague would not have supported her so enthusiastically or so quickly, and would have given more thought to other, comparable candidates, but on the other hand, if she were a little less meritorious or if another candidate were clearly, obviously superior, he would have not supported her no matter what animals she owns. We can also imagine a scenario in which your colleague's love of dogs is enough to produce such wishful thinking in him that even if the candidate was a few notches less meritorious than the others, he would overrate her work. Did Simon yell at me because he hates me or because he was drunk? Perhaps the drink only served to remove an inhibition or two, thus unleashing his deep hatred of me, or perhaps he does not hate me at all, and due to a drunken state, I am being yelled at for reasons that have nothing to do with me, or even with real hostility. This is why sometimes, when a person acts in a certain way while drunk, we say "Wow, he is showing his true colors," while at other times we say "Never mind him, it's only the drink talking." These are distinctions we have to deal with in dealing with self and others: distinctions not between the reasonable and the unreasonable, but between the ordinarily unreasonable and the worse-than-ordinarily unreasonable.

It is important here to note that *simply* the fact that a purely atavistic factor, like a drug, is involved in the causal circumstance of an action does not make it irrational. The atavistic factor only makes one irrational if it prevents one from acting for some good rationalizing reasons. Some atavistic factors do not do that: in fact, they *fight those factors that would prevent one from acting for good reasons*, and in this way *enhance the efficacy of* one's rationalizing reasons. Consider the following cases:

1. *Coffee!* Jamie's ability to respond to reasons is much higher when he is under the influence of caffeine. It is 2 P.M., and Jamie decides that it is too late for him to drink coffee, and so he orders a decaffeinated latte. Unbeknownst to him, the barista confuses his order and hands him a "real," caffeinated latte instead. At 2:30 P.M., Jamie attends a department meeting in which complex situations are outlined and intelligent decisions called for. Jamie

makes very good, perfectly rational decisions: needless to say, he makes them for the right reasons. He does not know, however, that if it were not for the mistake in the coffee shop, he would not have been so rational.

2. *Serotonin reuptake.* Joanna had good rationalizing reasons to quit her job. If it were not for these reasons, she would not have quit her job. But it is also true that if she were not on a sophisticated antidepressant, she would never have had the courage to do it. Assuming that the antidepressant worked as antidepressants are supposed to work, what it does is not make things look better than they are or reduce Joanna's inhibitions so that all of her hidden desires can motivate her more than before, but rather restore some rationality to a mind whose reason-responsiveness has been compromised by depression.

What is true of atavistic factors is also true of "mere content" factors. Thus consider the story of Julia. Julia had good rationalizing reasons to quit her job too. Like Joanna, if it were not for these reasons, Julia would not have quit. But if she were not in a happy romantic relationship, which cured her of some pesky insecurities for the time being, she would never have had the courage and presence of mind to quit.

ARE MENTAL DISORDERS JUST LIKE DIABETES?

The concept of a mental disorder presents some puzzles to people who write on freedom, reason responsiveness, and responsibility, and paradoxically enough it is in some ways *more* puzzling if one is a materialist about the mind than if one is not. It is common enough at present to hold that the difference between the person who is normal and the person who has a mental disorder is that the person who has a mental disorder has a physical illness. As one cliché goes, "It is just like having diabetes." A mental disorder, such as depression, causes mental states different from normal mental states in that depression is a physical or biochemical entity. But if one is a materialist about the mind, saying that a mental disorder is a state of the brain is saying something true, but not saying much. If the mental can be reduced to the physical, then all mental states are, at bottom, physical states, states of the brain. Love is a state of the brain, knowing psychiatry is a state of the brain, being a Republican is a state of the brain, the person who believes that it is now three in the morning is in a different state of the brain from the state of the brain of the person who believes it is now four in the morning, and so on. "Depression is an illness like diabetes" would be a fairly trivial claim if all we meant by it is that depression is a biochemical state, for so are love, Republicanism, and every other human mental state.

In a way, to say that depression is "just like" diabetes because both are states of the body is like saying that a software problem is "just like" a hardware problem because they are both states of the computer. No one claims that computers are anything but physical things. Still, if my computer fails to find a certain book at the Brown library, it could be a hardware problem, it could be a software problem, or it could be a "reality problem"—that is, simply the result of the fact that the Brown library does not have the book. Note that software problems often have hardware solutions: any programmer will tell you that often the best thing to do when your software fails is to turn the computer off and on again.

A materialist, then, cannot take literally the colloquial distinctions between "mental" and "biological." But even if we are materialists, we can, of course, make a distinction between the mental and the non-mental. Let us take a paradigmatic physical problem—say, a brain tumor—and a paradigmatic mental problem—say, dissatisfaction with a dreadful boss. Without committing ourselves to any particular view of the mental, it seems plausible that the causal circumstances that led to the brain tumor do not involve content efficacy, while the causal circumstances that led to the dissatisfaction with one's boss do involve content efficacy—perhaps even reason responsiveness, as one can be dissatisfied with a boss for good reasons.

In this section, I spend some time applying the distinctions just made between kinds of mental causes to instances of mental disorder. The purpose is twofold: first, the theory I have been developing of reason responsiveness could use further support, and showing that it illuminates some subtle issues in the understanding of mental disorders is a way of providing that support; and second, any theory of praise- and blameworthiness needs to have something to say about the moral (and other) worth of acts committed by those with mental disorders. In particular, my view, focused as it is on the quality of will of the agent, needs to have something sufficiently subtle to say about acts committed by people with mental disorders. Fortunately for me, such subtle commitments are a natural consequence of my view of reason responsiveness.

What, then, about conditions currently known as mental disorders? It seems that some of them are diabetes-like, some are very much not so, and others have diabetes-like components as well as components that involve some content efficacy. As I have said earlier, the three forms of causation— diabetes-like, merely content efficacious, and reason-responsive—are woven fine in complicated ways, and it would often be hard to explain a mental state without referring to all kinds. This is true even in cases in which we might be tempted to think that an individual's mental state is completely explainable in meaningful and reasoned terms and even in cases in which we might think that a "hardware" explanation is plainly sufficient for explaining the person's mental state. Let us look first at cases in which it might seem, at first, that reason responsiveness and content efficacy provide us all the explanation we can get. A person who is anxious because there is talk of downsizing in her company is reason-responsive—it is quite likely if we have reason to think that just about anyone in her situation would be anxious. However, it can be true that she would have been a little less anxious if some factors that are not reason responsive or are even contentless were different. Perhaps, for example, she imagines losing her job as more dangerous to her than it is, because of memories of her father losing his job, though she knows that he was in a different field, in a different era, with a different set of skills. Perhaps the amount of anxiety experienced by a person exposed to a stressful event depends, other things being equal, on her hard-wired temperament, and our tense worker is partially right to wish she were born with "nerves of steel" like some people are.

Now turn to a situation in which it seems that a reason-free, meaning-free, hardwired explanation might be all we need. Suppose we have a reason to believe that a person's hard-wiring would have made it very likely, under most circumstances, that she would at some point have serious problems with anxiety and insomnia. Suppose further that the person in question is anxious to the point of insomnia and anxious about something that most people would not be anxious about: perhaps the person, a middle-class American, is worried about famine in Africa. Suppose also the person's view on famine in Africa is not a completely unreasonable one and is shared by many normal people not made anxious as a result. In this case, it seems tempting to say that the anxiety is not a product of content-efficacious causation at all—it is the product of a "hard-wired" anxiety disorder. But we must not forget that there are many people with anxiety disorders to whom it has never occurred to worry about famine in Africa. It is perfectly possible that even if the person's propensity toward maladaptive anxiety is hardwired, the fact that he is anxious *about famine in Africa* rather than about the state of his bank account or the opinions of his friends on the subject of his appearance might very well have a content-oriented explanation. It might be true that if it weren't for hunger in Africa, he would be likely to worry about something anyway: but that does not make it an accident that the subject of his worry turned out to be hunger in Africa.

But some mental disorders are clearly more diabetes-like than others, in the sense that some of them display less content efficacy and reason responsiveness than others. With some disorders, we might need to amass more knowledge before knowing the extent to which there is content efficacy in them. To make things even more complicated, it is quite possible that some depressed people, for example, are more like diabetics than others—different cases of depression seem to run from the very meaningful to the starkly random—or that the content of some psychotic episodes is more accidental than the content of others (recall the two interpretations of the manic Hemingway).

For a clear appreciation of the differing roles that content can play in mental disorders, contrast the implications of telling a person that her colleague has Narcissistic Personality Disorder and the implications of telling a person that her colleague has Tourette Syndrome. Tourette Syndrome is a lot like diabetes, it seems. The knowledge that a person's behavior—say, his shouting of obscenities—is the result of Tourette Syndrome carries the important information that what seems content-efficacious behavior is in fact not so: it is in fact like diabetes symptoms, or coughs, or seizures (Schroeder forthcoming). Usually, a person who yells obscenities is moved by such things as hatred, hostility, or lack of concern for the sensibilities of the people around him, but in the case of the Tourettic person no such conclusion needs to be drawn. "It's not that she really hates you, or really wants to insult you. It's just a disease," we say, relieved. Telling a person that her colleague's arrogant and selfish behavior is the result of "Narcissistic Personality Disorder" is much less a clear affair. Here are the official diagnostic criteria for Narcissistic Personality Disorder (American Psychiatric Association 2000, 300.89): A pervasive pattern of grandiosity (in fantasy or behavior), need for admiration, and lack of empathy, beginning by early adulthood and present in a variety of contexts, as indicated by five (or more) of the following:

(1) has a grandiose sense of self-importance (e.g., exaggerates achievements and talents, expects to be recognized as superior without commensurate achievements)

(2) is preoccupied with fantasies of unlimited success, power, brilliance, beauty, or ideal love

(3) believes that he or she is "special" and unique and can only be understood by, or should associate with, other special or high-status people (or institutions)

(4) requires excessive admiration

(5) has a sense of entitlement, i.e., unreasonable expectations of especially favorable treatment or automatic compliance with his or her expectations

(6) is interpersonally exploitative, i.e., takes advantage of others to achieve his or her own ends

(7) lacks empathy: is unwilling to recognize or identify with the feelings and needs of others

(8) is often envious of others or believes that others are envious of him or her

(9) shows arrogant, haughty behaviors or attitudes

To have these traits, then, is to have Narcissistic Personality Disorder. In the case of the narcissist, we cannot truly say "it's not that he really is indifferent to the needs of others; it's only a disease like diabetes," or "it's not that he really thinks he is superior to you; it's only a disease like diabetes." The narcissist *does* think he is superior to you. He *is* indifferent to the needs of others. The usual content-efficacious causes for arrogant and selfish behavior are in fact behind his arrogant and selfish behavior (while the usual content-efficacious causes of swearing do not exist in the Tourettic person; again, see Schroeder forthcoming). It is clear enough what we mean when we compare the Tourettic person's swearing to diabetes (or sneezes, or seizures). It is not clear what we mean when we compare the narcissist's slighting of his colleagues to any of these things. As a result, labeling someone with the official term "Narcissistic Personality Disorder" is hardly any less derogatory than simply calling someone "a narcissist" or "a selfish, self-absorbed megalomaniac." Note that if we were to prove that the narcissist's behavior is a way of compensating for deep insecurity, we might consider it a bit more forgivable, but we would not make it the contentless thing like a sneeze or a seizure, or even the semicontentful thing that is a bout of anxiety.

What are we to make of all this? It seems to me that, for the moral psychologist, there are two cautionary conclusions to draw. One concerns meaningfulness; the other concerns moral responsibility.

First, meaningfulness: Imagine an artist who spends long, excited nights in a state of inspiration which results in good art. Imagine this artist being told that his state of inspiration is actually a borderline form of mania known as 'hypomania' (American Psychiatric Association 2000, under

"Mood Disorders," 296.89), and that hypomania is a symptom of a disease, just like a diabetes-induced seizure or the ravings of Tourettic person. Or imagine the person who is anxious about hunger in Africa told that his losing sleep over hunger in Africa is likewise a symptom of a disease just like diabetes. If his art is central to the life or identity of the artist or social conscience central to the life and identity of the anxious person, such statements are likely to make them feel either insulted or devastated: a natural reaction to being told that the meaningful activities and concerns of your life are like sneezes. The artist might doubt his art is meaningful; the socially conscious insomniac might be deprived of his confidence that caring about things like hunger in Africa makes him at least a somewhat good person. But there is no reason for them to be devastated, and there is good reason for them to be insulted. While the fact that one is prone to hypomanic episodes is a brute "hardware" fact, it is probably no accident that the artist spends his hypomanic times creating rather than doing things that other hypomanics do: shopping, gambling, or having sex. It is probably also not an accident that he produces a certain kind of art and not another, and that his art is good rather than bad. The meaningfulness of the art is not necessarily reduced by the fact that it was created by a hypomanic any more than it would be reduced if we were to hear that it was created under the influence of three shots of strong espresso. Likewise for the anxious person.

The cautionary conclusion with regard to meaning is that one cannot assume that a mental state or apparent action is meaningless just because it is part of, or an expression of, a state that is classified—even for good reasons—as a mental disorder. Whether or not what we have here is "like diabetes"—or to what extent it is—varies from disorder to disorder and often from case to case, and at times it makes sense to suspend some judgments until either more empirical data are available about the condition or more knowledge is gathered about the life of the person in question. The cautionary conclusion with regard to moral responsibility is similar: the fact that a person is regarded as mentally ill does not automatically mean that she not blameworthy or praiseworthy. Whether or not she is or to what extent she is depends on the particular combination of the diabetes-like on the one hand and the strange but perfectly contentful on the other.

Thus, while many mental disorders do seem to provide exempting, excusing, or mitigating conditions, some do not, and with others things are complicated. Of those disorders that do not serve as mitigating conditions, most famous, of course, is the condition of those who used to be called "morally insane," then psychopaths or sociopaths, and now sufferers from

Antisocial Personality Disorder. To say that someone has Antisocial Personality Disorder is essentially to say that she is what philosophers call an "amoralist," a person lacking in moral concern and at times (as in the case of a homicidal maniac) overflowing with ill will. It is essentially to say that the person in question is so bad that, unlike other bad people, she does not have the occasional pang of conscience. This is tacitly acknowledged by the law in that when such persons commit crimes, they are not exempt from punishment due to their deviance: their deviance simply *is* being unusually bad. Then, more interestingly, there are the cases of which one does not know what to think.

For a complicated case, consider Factitious Disorder. "Factitious Disorder" is the current term for the condition of a person who goes to extremes in order to pretend to be sick, or to induce real, painful, and sometimes dangerous physical symptoms in herself, for no tangible benefits except for receiving emotional support from others. Even when such a person pretends rather than induces symptoms, she often risks herself because she subjects herself to risky and painful medical procedures of the kind that are performed when the origin of a person's symptoms remains a mystery for too long. At times, the person clearly refuses any benefits other than sympathy: one person described by Feldman, Ford, and Reinhold in *Patient or Pretender* (1995, 1–19) pretended to have cancer, starving herself and cutting her hair, and continuously refused to apply for benefits or to accept offers of extra time from her boss and colleagues. These obvious potential gains were nothing to her by comparison to the additional sympathy and respect she received for constantly refusing them. What is one to think of a person like that? Reading cases, one alternates between feeling sorry for the miserable loneliness that seems to drive some people to such extremes to rage at the horrible wrong done to the people who are emotionally manipulated by the pretender and, in some cases, at the wasted medical resources. The balance between "desperate cry for help" reactions and "manipulative bastards" reactions varies with the details of each case, though it veers decisively to one side in the very rare cases of what is called "Munchausen Syndrome by Proxy" (Feldman, Ford, Reinhold, 131–146)—when a parent makes her child sick and subjects her to endless medical procedures just to gain the role of the martyred parent. We might be tempted to call this person crazy, because unlike, say, a person who commits a white-collar crime, her motives are very strange: even very selfish people would often rather not spend all their time around hospitals. But the strangeness does not eliminate the sense of sickening selfishness that these people evoke, even in the psychiatrists who attempt to change them.

Again, the question here is not whether, someday, someone might come up with a pill that can change these behaviors, as, if materialism is true, some type of pill could in principle change just about any mental state. Whether we are discussing deviant mental conditions or ordinary mental conditions, it seems that if we wish to be materialists about the mind, we need to pay close attention to the things that make some mental states different from others, and one of these things is reason responsiveness.

MORAL RESPONSIBILITY–INCOMPATIBILISM WITHOUT ROMANTIC-INCOMPATIBILISM?

Suppose a romantic incompatibilist becomes reformed. She decides to withdraw her claims that true love, true art, true scientific achievement, and so on are meaningless in a deterministic world. She decides to agree openly that we respond to reasons in a deterministic world. She insists, however, on remaining an incompatibilist on one specific issue: moral responsibility. In a deterministic world, she says, you could be smart and prudent, loving and compassionate, all kinds of good things. What you cannot be is morally praiseworthy or blameworthy.

This is the position taken by the hard determinist Derk Pereboom in *Living without Free Will* (2001). Pereboom presents arguments against the claim that one can be morally responsible in a determined setting, but he also insists that his arguments do not extend to reason responsiveness. After all, he says, for us to act for reasons, all that is needed is that our actions be caused by psychological states that are reasons for them, and that is possible in a deterministic world as well. (Pereboom presumably thinks of causation by reasons in Fischer-esque and Davidson-like ways, but he could use the same argument using my version—i.e., he could have said, "For us to act for reasons all we need is that our actions be caused by psychological states that are rationalizing reasons for them by virtue of that which makes them such rationalizing reasons.")

But can he really get rid of praiseworthiness and blameworthiness without getting rid of reason-responsiveness as well? Let us take a look at what I take to be Pereboom's key example, Professor Plum. In Pereboom's original version, Plum is micromanaged by neuroscientists, minute by minute, neuron by neuron: "Suppose these neuroscientists 'locally' manipulate him to undertake the process of reasoning by which his desires are brought about and modified—directly producing his every state from moment to moment" (2001, 112–13). Pereboom takes it that if, in this way, the neuro-scientists "get" Plum to deliberate and reason as to whether to kill Ms. White, to decide to kill Ms. White, and then do it, Plum would not be blameworthy for the killing. Pereboom thinks that this must be because Plum's actions are determined (this is a first step in an argument in which Pereboom hopes to show that those of us who are determined in more subtle ways than Plum is are in the same boat). According to Pereboom, it must be true that Plum is blameless because his actions and thoughts are determined by the scientists: It cannot be because he does not respond to reason, because for all we know, he does: his creators cause his states one by one in the same way in which they would occur if he were reasoning. Thus, to give a simplistic example, if Plum thought "all men are stupid" and "George is a man," the neuroscientists would quickly induce in him the thought "George is stupid" exactly because the two earlier thoughts are good rationalizing reasons to think "George is stupid."

But would that really be reason-responsiveness? If anything, Mr. Plum is exactly the sort of deviant chain story that can be used against theories of reason responsiveness. If one says, as Pereboom does, that reason re-sponsivness is what occurs when the thought "this is too loud" causes me to turn down the radio, an objector may come in with a story like Plum's—a neuroscientist creates the impulse to turn on the radio as a response to Plum's thought "it's loud"—and bring it as a counter example: "surely you don't think this is reason responsiveness, do you?" In fact, this is the kind of story that I did not regard as my obligation to answer because not only is it an objection to theories of reason responsiveness: what we have here is a deviant causal chain scenario of the sort that can wreak metaphysical havoc with any story in which causation is involved, reasons or not (such as the story "the rock broke the window"). It is not clear that Plum acts for reasons, it is not even clear that he moves for mental causes, and it is not clear if he is a person at all. Thus, Pereboom would be pressed to show us that it is the determined nature of Plum's "action" that makes him appear nonblameworthy, as opposed to his lack of reason responsiveness. It is hard to see why determinism would take away praiseworthiness, blameworthi-ness, good and ill will—without taking away reason-responsiveness and meaningful will in general, In a world in which we can respond to reasons, including rather complicated sorts of reasons, it would be hard to explain why moral reasons would be the only exception.

Ought Implies Can?
An Argumemt from Epistemology

Suppose I raise my arm, perhaps in order to demonstrate to my students a point about raising my arm. I want to raise my arm, and I do so quite consciously. My muscles obey me and the process is problem free. As I raise my arm, I have a clear sense of freedom: a sense that if I hadn't wanted to raise my arm, I would not have done it, that I am free to bring my arm back to where it was, that whether or not I raise my arm is *up to me*. I raise my arm "under the idea of freedom," as Kant would say. I wish to call this thing that I experience myself as having when I thus raise my arm 'arm-raising freedom', or 'AR freedom' for short. In many ways, AR freedom is paradigmatic freedom. The experience of AR freedom seems to be the most elementary experience at the base of our sense that, in some way or another, we have free will.

Let us imagine a smart undergraduate student who is interested in the free will problem and its implication. In homage to Strawsonian terminology, we can call him Paul the Pessimist. Paul used to think that he has free will, for he seemed to exercise it in raising his arm. When he started suspecting that determinism might be true, he started suspecting that if determinism is true, there is no free will after all. If this is the case, he reasons, the experience he has when he raises his arm must be an illusion, just as Spinoza (1674)[1] says it is, for surely, if determinism is true, then I could not have done otherwise, and if I could not have done otherwise, there can be no sense in which whether or not I raise my arm is up to me. In this way, Paul can be said to accept the basic insight at the root of van Inwagen's "Consequence Argument" (1975).

Imagine that Paul is introduced to the simple compatibilist view advanced by A. J. Ayer ([1954] 1980). "Look," says Olga the Optimist, who likes Ayer's

---

[1] In response to his correspondent's claim that he can freely choose whether to write his letter or not, Spinoza speculates that even a falling rock, if conscious and ignorant of gravity,

view, "even in a deterministic world, you still raise your arm freely, because the raising of your arm is caused by your own wanting to raise your arm. When you say that you could have done otherwise, you are merely indicating that if you had wanted to do otherwise, you would have done otherwise, that no one held a gun to your head, and so on. This is true of you, while it is not true of a person who is tied to a chair. What more can you ask for, when it comes to free will?" As anyone who has taught undergraduates about free will can attest, Paul is likely to find this reply a cold comfort, at best. His answer to the optimist is likely to be the following: "But you don't understand. If determinism is true, it might be true that I chose to raise my arm in the sense that my raising my arm was caused by my wanting to raise my arm, but it is still true that I did not *choose to want* to raise my arm. Environmental factors and genetic factors made it impossible for me not to want to raise my arm at this moment. It was predetermined by the initial state of the world and the laws of nature that I should want to raise my arm, and want it enough to be led to decision and action. So despite my sense of control, I am no more than a puppet in the hand of these influences." Olga may point out that perhaps, for example, while Paul did not chose to desire to raise his arm, he may have chosen to act on the desire: but Paul is likely to shrug this off: and who chose the desire to act on the desire? Paul's conviction might only become stronger when he contemplates examples involving moral responsibility. "Robert Harris chose to commit murder," he might say, "but he didn't choose to want to commit murder. His extreme early childhood experiences and his later experiences in youth prison, as well as subtler factors, made it inevitable that he would hate his fellow human beings, lack moral concern or moral convictions, and want to commit murder. Thus, he is not morally responsible." Olga might then answer that it does not matter whether or not Harris chose to be a bad person with murderous desires: he might not be responsible for the fact that he is a bad person with murderous desires, but he *is* responsible for the murder he committed. Paul is likely to remain unconvinced.

Paul and Olga demonstrate something that is often overlooked in more sophisticated, professional discussions of free will and moral responsibility. They demonstrate that much of the argument between compatibilism and incompatibilism concerns the following question: does it or does it not

---

would be likely to experience itself as free. I still find his discussion of AR freedom one of the best.

matter, for the purpose of moral responsibility and other normative questions, whether or not we have chosen our mental states? Paul and Olga disagree on the question of whether, for the purposes of moral responsibility, we need to have freely chosen not only our actions, but also freely come by the beliefs, desires, and other attitudes that led to these actions. A philosophically sophisticated Olga might try to accommodate Paul's intuition by offering more nuanced versions of compatibilism. She might, for example, suggest, as per early Frankfurt (1971), that what really matters is whether our lower-order desires are endorsed by our higher-order desires, or she might suggest, as per my own view, that what really matters is whether our actions reflect good will, ill will, or indifference. Paul, ultimately, will not be satisfied: as long as your higher-order desires, ill will, and the like, were made inevitable by genetic and environmental factors, you are not free and therefore not responsible.

There is one strange (though not necessarily damning) thing in Paul's otherwise very commonsensical argument. Paul's notion of freedom—an "alternate possibilities" notion—has its pre-theoretical beginning in the experience of AR (arm-raising) freedom. Paul then goes on to say that if determinism is true, I did not raise my arm freely, because I did not choose to *want* to raise my arm. Similarly, Robert Harris did not commit murder freely, because he did not chose to have a desire to murder people. But we do not have paradigmatic experiences of AR freedom that concern "choosing to want." Sitting in class, Paul has doubtless asked himself many times whether or not to raise his hand in response to a teacher's question and experienced himself clearly and simply as choosing to raise his hand or not raise it. Most probably, he has never asked himself whether or not *to want* to raise his hand and never experienced himself as choosing to want to raise his hand or not want to raise his hand.

The compelling experience that leads one to believe that one has free will in the first place, the experience of AR freedom, generally involves actions, not desires (or beliefs, or preferences, or feelings). If I want to raise my arm, I raise my arm. If I want *to want* to visit my uncle, this does not result in my having that desire; it might result in my attempting, successfully or unsuccessfully, to induce the desire in myself—perhaps via drugs or therapy or hypnosis or muttering "I love my uncle" many times under my breath. What I would be doing or attempting to do is analogous not to raising one's arm, but to using all kinds of mental techniques to cause one's penis to become erect or to induce tears in one's eyes. One does not will an erection (or having an erection would be an action). One can induce an erection, and sometimes, often with a lot more effort, one can induce in oneself a desire to see one's uncle. Of course, it happens that instrumental desires spring spontaneously from intrinsic desires and beliefs: I want some quiet and as a result I want to throw my yowling cat out of the room. In this case I might say, "I wanted some quiet, and so I decided to throw the cat out of the room" or "I wanted some quiet, and for that reason I wanted to throw the cat out of the room." But note that if we assume anything like a normal case, I will not say, "I wanted some quiet, and so I *decided to want* to throw my cat out of the room." However slow, deliberative, reflective, and introspective I am—and I am the sort of person who occasionally makes a conscious decision to raise her arm! —I do not experience myself as "deciding to want" to do it.

Note also that what I have said does not apply merely to first-order desires; it applies to desires of any order. Imagine that Lynn has a desire for chocolate, a desire to not have a desire for chocolate (because it's fattening), a desire not to have a desire to not have a desire for chocolate (because she wants not to bow to contemporary standards of beauty) and a desire not to have the previous desire (because she hates being such a complicated person). The three higher-order desires did not come into existence by decision or willing any more than the first-order desire for chocolate did.

None of this refutes Paul's view, of course, nor does it refute the claim that there might still be some sort of freedom that we have over our desires. But it worth beginning with the observation that while our idea of paradigmatic free will stems from the experience of AR freedom, when Paul says that in order to attribute freedom to the arm raiser we need to assume that wanting to raise her arm was also up to her, we talk about a putative freedom that does not come with that experience.

A related anomaly has to do with Paul's conviction that the arm raiser cannot be praiseworthy or blameworthy for raising her arm unless she is somehow responsible for wanting to raise her arm. Suppose, for example, that I raised my arm because I wanted to do the right thing, and in context, I thought raising my arm was the right thing (I am, say, voting). By Paul's reasoning, it appears that I cannot be praiseworthy for raising my arm unless somehow not only raising my arm but wanting to raise my arm is up to me. This is, prima facie, a little awkward. Assume, for example, that an agent can only be praiseworthy for an action if the action is performed out of good will, or—to make things simple—from duty, or the desire to do the right thing. We can call that, for economy's sake, "acting out of duty." But even according to Kant there is no such thing as a duty to act for the sake of duty. To be sure, we have related duties: a duty to do the right thing, that which the moral law dictates to us; a duty to do our best to instill good will or dutifulness in ourselves and our children; a duty to do our best to develop in ourselves inclinations that would make us more likely to do things that we have a duty to do.[2] There is nothing wrong with the idea of a duty to develop in ourselves devotion to duty, but a duty to act from duty would be a category mistake. If we had a duty to act from duty, then acting from duty would itself be right action, which we would have a duty to perform, which would mean that one could ask whether an agent acted out of duty (*a*) out of duty or (*b*) merely out of inclination. It would likewise raise the question of whether the agent's acting out of good will was a demonstration of good will on her part or not. Questions about third-order and higher-order dutifulness and good will would also be raised. There is, however, no need for such questions. The moral worth of an individual's good action depends on our evaluation of the individual's motive or will. The motive or will is good in itself, as Kant holds (1964). Thus the Kantian agent, when faced with, say, a child about to drown, is expected to go and do his duty—helping the child—and *not worry about his motives*. This insight is not restricted to Kant and his followers, either. The Talmud, similarly, states that doing the good for its own sake or for love of the good is superior to doing it for other motives, but its advice to the reader who scrutinizes his motives and sees that he has no love of the good is not to love the good or else. The advice is to go ahead and do the good, for whatever motives, and the right motives will come eventually. Actions can be prescribed, but the motives for them cannot.

If we think of the moral law as ordering us to do things, we can see that there are things that it makes sense to order and things that it does not. You might want your child to play the piano willingly, or to play the piano for its own sake, or to play the piano "but not because I said so," but it makes little sense to give commands to these effects. It makes sense to say, "Play the piano, and I hope you do it willingly." It makes sense to say, "You should be the kind of person who likes playing the piano, so work on making yourself such a person." It also makes sense to complain behind the child's back, "Well, he plays the piano when I tell him, but he doesn't do it willingly or for its own sake." But this complaint is *not* a complaint about disobedience. If it were, we would end up asking if the child who plays the piano willingly does so willingly or otherwise. The distinction being

---

[2] Contrary to Schiller's notorious quip ([1793] 1983), if you are already inclined to help your friends, Kantianism does not tell you to destroy that inclination so you can act from the motive of duty instead.

discussed between things that can be ordered and things that cannot be ordered echoes the commonsensical distinction between actions and the motives behind actions; it also seems to echo the distinction between things that come with a sense of AR freedom and things that do not.

These considerations are drawing us once again to conclusions incompatible with Paul's. Paul insists that we must be in control of our motives for action, and not merely in control of our actions, if we are to be free, praiseworthy, or blameworthy. But ethical thought and common sense have generally held that our motives are not chosen in any sense, much less chosen freely. And certainly I need ethical thought and common sense to be right in this matter, if my own theory of praise- and blameworthiness is to withstand Paul's challenge. But I suspect that Paul and his fellow incompatibilists will not be moved by the data of ethical theory and common sense that I have just presented. A number of objections remain open to them, including an objection from an apparently very basic ethical datum: the dictum that *ought* implies *can*. Following Peter van Inwagen (1983), an incompatibilist about moral responsibility might present the following argument:

1. If I am morally obligated not to *x*, then I ought to have acted otherwise.
But 2. Ought implies can.
3. If determinism is true, my course of action is not up to me. It is inevitable. Thus, it is not true that I ought to have acted otherwise.
4. If it is not true that I ought to have acted in a certain way, I cannot be blameworthy for not having acted in a certain way.[3]
Thus,
5. If determinism is true, I am not praiseworthy or blameworthy for my action.

I propose to take the radical step of arguing that (2) is false. Ought does not imply can.

BELIEF AND CHOICE

There are important differences between norms that apply to actions and norms that apply to desires, beliefs, and other attitudes that feature in the causal chain that, in a deterministic world, lead to action. With regard to

---

[3] I take it to be an intuition that in order for me to be blameworthy for an action, it has to be the case that the action is wrong. For a fascinating attempt to attack this intuition, see the work of Haji (1998, 2002).

actions, I favor the standard compatibilist substitute for the thought that 'ought' implies 'can': one ought to take a course of action only if it is true that if one wanted to take this course of action, one could do so. When it comes to attitudes like beliefs and desires, as opposed to actions, nothing like "ought implies can" applies. If we are to assess a person's will itself as good or bad, it does not matter at all whether the person could have wanted otherwise or not. If this is correct, a compatibilist can accept some version of the view that an action is praiseworthy or blameworthy if it springs from certain motives—be it my version or another one—without worrying about whether or not the motives themselves happened to occur in the agent as the inevitable result of genetic and environmental factors.

Duty epistemologists argue that since epistemology is normative, it must be true that belief formation is something over which we have freedom. I reverse their argument and argue that while epistemology is normative, we have no freedom over belief formation (i.e., we cannot "believe otherwise" than we do), and therefore it is possible for normative truths to apply to things over which we have no freedom.

I take it to be obvious that there are genuine epistemic norms, that there is epistemic rationality and epistemic irrationality. In one academic institution I attended, a student wrote on an exam that Homer lived in the first century. When asked why she thought so, she said, "The professor said that Homer was the *first* Greek poet, so I gather he must have lived in the *first* century." Assuming (as I fear was true) that the student in question knew just as much as her peers about the way time is recorded, and could, for instance, explain the concept of "before Christ" if you asked her to do so, I take it that the student in question *ought to have known better*, that she made an inference that *she should not have made*. It is also fair to say that she has good *reasons* for not believing that Homer lived in the first century and that in making her inference she *failed to respond to epistemic reasons*.

So epistemology is normative. There is no particular reason, however, to think of all these normative facts as necessitating the existence of duties to *do* anything. For my own part, it seems obvious that epistemology is normative and that we have no control over our beliefs. But I will say a little more about this before going on, for those to whom it is less obvious.

Consider the first reason people generally give for thinking that we have no choice over what to believe, or for thinking that the burden of proof lies on the epistemic voluntarists. This is the absence of AR freedom experienced with regard to our beliefs. While it is normally easy to raise your arm by choice, it normally appears impossible to change a belief by similar choice. If a man with a gun says "hands up," one raises one's hands without difficulty. On the other hand, if I were threatened with death unless I started believing that two plus two equals five, or that Providence is the capital of the United States, or that my eye color is more of a light hazel than a dark brown, I would not be able to do so. All the motivation in the world would not suffice to change my beliefs in such circumstances. If I had, say, a pill that was likely to make me believe that two plus two equals five, I could, of course, take it, but this again would not be like choosing to raise one's arm: it would be like choosing to hit one's arm with a reflex hammer that would cause it to jerk upward.

Let us suppose for the sake of the argument that it is true that we have no AR freedom over our actions. Alston (1993) and others think that if this much is true, one simply has to give up the idea that epistemology is normative. If our beliefs are as much under our control as cell metabolism and the secretion of gastric juices, how can they be normative?

This is where my previous discussion of reason responsiveness becomes relevant. The important difference between cell metabolism and the development of beliefs is not in the presence or the absence of some type of control but rather in the fact that one of these processes is reason-responsive and one is not. Cell metabolism is not responsive to reasons—it is what was referred to earlier as a robot process. On the other hand, the development of beliefs is generally a reason-responsive process (though not universally so, of course). I argued earlier that unless one denies the existence of content efficacy, one cannot assume that choice or control or freedom are necessary for reason responsiveness to take place; that argument can be made, mutatis mutandis, for epistemic reason responsiveness as readily as for practical reason responsiveness.

This point can be illustrated by looking at one of Mattias Steup's comparisons between belief and action (2001). Steup points out that there are some cases in which we *act* for good reasons and have no choice in the matter. He mentions a case in which overwhelming prudential and moral considerations compel you to step on the brakes of your car. In this case, he points out, you cannot do otherwise, nor for that matter do you have the experience of freedom anymore than you do over believing that two plus two equals four. You are pushed to action by the very fact that you have those overwhelming reasons. Yet, we do not deny that you ought (morally and prudentially) to step on your brakes. Steup holds that if we can say such a thing about an action, we can say the same thing about beliefs. If we have a compatibilist view of freedom, he says, we hold that we have freedom or control over our actions whenever we act for good

reasons, and not, say, as a result of a compulsion. Thus, if we have a compatibilist view of freedom, then we must agree that we have freedom over both
the action and the belief, because both of them are the result of reasons. If
we have a stringent libertarian view of freedom, Steup says, then we have
no reason not to regard both the belief and the action as something with
respect to which we have no choice or control. Either way, the belief and
the action are in the same boat.

The similarity between the belief case and the action case is something
that should be taken to heart. In both cases, there is reason responsiveness
and in both cases, there seems to be no "modal" freedom—no ability to do
otherwise—and also no experience of AR freedom. Unlike Steup, however,
what I have been arguing for is *not* compatibilism about freedom, but compatibilism about reason-responsiveness. I am perfectly willing to think of
freedom in the traditional sense of selecting among alternative possibilities,
and perfectly willing to accept that if determinism is true, this is something
that we do not have either with respect to our beliefs or with respect to
our actions. In order to think that norms for both practical and theoretical
rationality apply to us, we need to believe that human beings are capable
of responding to moral and epistemic reasons; we do not necessarily need
freedom, however otherwise desirable it might be.

This can be obscured by the fact that colloquial ways of talking about
believing tend to be ambiguous between the vocabulary of freedom and
the vocabulary of reason responsiveness.[4] Consider the different uses of
such verbs as *agree* and *accept*. You can agree with a claim and agree to do
something, which makes an epistemic matter, agreeing with claims, sound
like a practical matter, agreeing to plans. There are some contexts in which
the two can seem interchangeable: if, for example, one is in a congressional
debate or is involved in a collective decision, it might matter very little if,
when I say, "I accept what my colleague said" I mean that I think he is
speaking the truth or that I agree to argue about this no further and to
follow his suggestions if they are approved by a majority. Even so, these
are different things altogether.

Consider also the celebrated remark by Eleanor Roosevelt, that no one
can make you feel inferior without your consent. Upon inquiry, more than
one therapist has told me that one of the most common problems that
leads a person who does not have a true mental disorder to see a therapist
is a sense of inferiority. If no one can make you feel inferior without your

---

[4] Not unlike the vocabulary of action (e.g., the use of the word *autonomatic* to mean both
'unchosen' and 'blind', or 'robotic').

consent, why are people paying so much money trying not to feel inferior? Why don't they simply refuse to consent? It strikes me as unnecessarily florid and far-fetched to speculate that all of them, deep down, really want to feel inferior in some way or another. It is much more reasonable to say that no, one *can* be made to feel inferior without one's consent. There is a more charitable reading of Roosevelt's remark, though: that people cannot make you feel inferior simply by saying that you are or treating you as if you are unless you have some feelings and beliefs that you already share with them. For example, no one can make you feel significantly inferior by making fun of your taste in clothes unless at some level you feel or believe that your taste in clothes is very important, and that the judgments of others carry some weight when it comes to clothing. As a result, two different people might listen to the same devastating critique of their clothing and one of them might feel inferior and the other one might not, and in this sense it is true that one doesn't *have* to feel inferior, from whence comes a useful bit of advice—which is probably the real reason some people regard the quote as inspirational—that if a person makes you feel inferior, you should examine the beliefs or other attitudes that make it possible for that person to make you feel inferior, and perhaps you'll discover that some of them are silly, and then you can feel better. The truth of the claim that all cases of feeling inferior have such a character is doubtful, perhaps, but I take it to be much closer to the truth than the view that feeling inferior is a matter of choice.

There are, of course, phenomena that might be loosely referred to as instances of freedom over one's beliefs or choosing to believe. These phenomena are real, but they are not really cases in which one has freedom or choice regarding beliefs. Surveying them will further support the idea that epistemic 'oughts' apply in the absence of epistemic 'cans'.

Change of belief due to reflection. Imagine that Uncle Duke of *Doonesbury* fame believes that there is a lizard before him. Then he starts to reflect. He wonders if he is really seeing the lizard or whether he is hallucinating. After examining the stash of recreational drugs in his room and discussing the matter with his nephew, he comes to the conclusion that he must have taken a hallucinogen. He goes back to bed and waits for the phantom lizard to go away. Retrospectively, he might say that he chose not to believe in the existence of the lizard.

Whether or not belief is something that we can decide to do, reflection is something that we can decide to do. One might choose to reflect on a question—anything from "Do we have any milk in the fridge?" to "What is the right way to interpret *Being and Time*?" and stop when one has either developed a belief or got tired of thinking. One can even, like Uncle Duke above, reflect oneself into disbelieving one's own eyes. This can all be true without there being any such thing as believing at will, because reflection, like fishing or fact finding, is a process which we can decide to initiate but whose results we cannot choose. Uncle Duke might not have chosen to reflect as to whether the lizard in front of him was real or not, but once he did, and once his reasoning provided him with the relevant evidence, he reached the conclusion that he must be on a hallucinogen, not because of his will, but because of the evidence considered. Of course, his exercise of his will (in deliberating) was causally important to reaching his conclusion, but it did not determine the conclusion: it only determined that a conclusion would be reached that took into account those pieces of evidence selected by him as worthy of deliberation. The conclusion itself was determined by the evidence he considered.

There are, of course, ways to manipulate the process of reflection—or any other belief-formation process—in such a way as to produce a certain outcome or make it more likely. This is what I wish to discuss next.

Manipulating one's belief-formation apparatus. Consider the case of Kermy, who suffers from schizoaffective disorder, a condition mixing elements of both schizophrenia and manic depression (American Psychiatric Association 2000, 295.70). He has been sleeping badly for a while. He starts experiencing a frightening agitated state, which he finds all too familiar. From his experience in the past he knows that if he allows this state to take its natural course, he will soon start having false and unpleasant beliefs. It is likely, he knows, that he will start believing that his family is plotting to poison him. Fortunately, Kermy has been well trained by a clever psychiatrist. As soon as he spots the agitation, he takes the large dose of risperidone that has been prescribed to him for this purpose. Thus, he does not come to believe that his family is going to poison him. He might say that he decided not to go through the hell of paranoid delusion: not to have false, paranoid beliefs.

What Kermy does here is not believe at will, but manipulate his belief-formation apparatus in such a way as to make the development a particular belief less likely. The capacity to do this accounts for a lot of phenomena. A psychotropic drug is a very obvious way to manipulate one's belief-forming apparatus, but another obvious (though often unsuccessful) way is staring into the mirror and saying, again and again, "I am beautiful," or "I think I can," or whatever else one wants to believe. Then there are things like attending church and hoping that somehow other people's belief in the existence of God might "rub off" on you. There are also many subtler, more complex ways for this kind of self-manipulation to be effected. Here are a few instances:

1. *Cover story.* Susan is a spy, and she trains, in the manner described in detail in John Le Carre's *Little Drummer Girl*, to infiltrate a group of terrorists, posing as a new recruit. The best spy, she knows, is the one who almost, but not quite, believes her lies while she tells them. Thus, she closely studies the social and psychological circumstances that would lead a person similar to her to join the group of terrorists. She immerses herself in the relevant militant literature, and uses hypertrophied "method acting" tricks to make her cover story as vivid to her as possible, enough to produce believable emotional reactions when "in character." The danger in such training, it is said, is that one can perform such suggestion so well that while behind enemy lines, it can take surprisingly little for the pseudo-beliefs to become true beliefs, and thus for the agent to turn over to the side of those on whom she is spying. Thus, in at least in susceptible people, this type of immersion can be used to induce real beliefs.

2. *Mood music.* Grace, a music lover, likes to play *The Mikado* before important days at work. Listening to the operetta, in which characters face a bizarre and unpredictable world in which they nonetheless manage to emerge victorious, tends to put her a certain mood—optimistic, but with an awareness of the absurdities of the world. In such a mood, she is likely, when considering any task which happens to be before her, to develop beliefs about her chances of success that are just a little bit more optimistic than the evidence warrants—which in turn increase her chances of success.

3. *Thought control.* Andrew is one of these people who have unusually good control over the direction of his conscious reflections. While on an airplane, he suddenly begins to doubt that he locked the door when he left his house. Not wishing to have to worry during his trip, he tells himself, "Stop that!" He quickly turns his mind to something else, and a moment later he forgets his doubt. He spends the rest of his trip as if the safety of his house were not in question. Later, he might describe doing so as having "chosen to believe" that everything is fine.

4. *Distraction tactics.* George, unlike Andrew, does not have much of an ability to order his mind to change its object of contemplation. While he sits in an airplane, he tells himself many times to "stop that," and yet he finds himself unable to escape wondering whether or not he locked the door. So

he tries a less direct method. He forces himself to read an unfamiliar book by his favorite mystery author. At the beginning he has trouble concentrating, but the book is a page turner, and so by the time he reaches page 15 he forgets his doubts about the door. He spends the rest of his trip as if the safety of his house were not in question.

5. *Suppressing evidence.* Laura is about to submit her dissertation on the subject of frogs, after a long struggle with perfectionism and the urge to revise. As she leafs through new issues of journals in her field, she spots an article whose title and first few lines suggest that there is some chance that it might contain findings that, if she reads them, will change her beliefs about frogs, which will result in a strong urge to revise her dissertation, just a little, yet again. Quickly, she puts the journal on the shelf with the others. She then puts the finished dissertation in her backpack, zips it up and proceeds to have some wine and watch television, resolved to push this incident out of her mind. The incident is forgotten by the next day, and her beliefs regarding frogs remain unchanged, though she might not be quite as certain of them as before.

In all of these cases, the agent does not choose to believe simpliciter, but rather chooses to tinker with her or his psychology indirectly, via taking direct actions making it more likely that certain beliefs develop and not others. In some cases, the agent performs this self-manipulation just as an unwanted belief is beginning to form in order to nip it in the bud; in others, an existing belief is suppressed out of existence before it has completely taken root—a form of self-deception. At other times the process is much longer and more complicated and elaborate.

Pure-hearted manipulation. Choosing to do something that makes you likely or unlikely to believe a true proposition, while also sometimes referred to as "choosing to believe," is again not really a case of choosing to believe at all. As Parfit pointed out, it can sometimes be rational to induce epistemic irrationality (1986). For example, if someone threatened to kill me unless I believed in his divinity, I might have a good reason to do something (take a drug) in order to make me believe in this person's divinity, and I might have a reason to do so exactly *because* I do not have what is ordinarily regarded as a good reason to believe in his divinity. But one has to be careful here. It is not the existence of an ulterior motive such as wishing to save one's life that makes the difference between reasons to believe and reasons to make yourself likely to believe. While in the examples above the agent chooses to induce or help to induce a belief in herself or himself for reasons of convenience, prudence, morality, or for therapeutic reasons, one can also manipulate one's belief-forming apparatus for the sake of making oneself more likely to believe the truth. Here are some cases:

1. *Turning coffee into theorems.* Paul Erdos, pure-heartedly seeking the solution to a mathematical problem, pours himself a cup of very strong coffee, with the intention of improving his powers of reasoning. As he is said to have quipped, "A mathematician is a machine for turning coffee into theorems."

2. *Hold that thought.* Mark is trying to discover the best possible interpretation of a difficult passage by Leibniz. At some point, he comes up with an interpretation that strikes him as very likely to be true. The hour is late and Mark is getting a little tired, but he is tempted to read Leibniz again, just to double check. From his experience, however, Mark knows that if he reads yet again the text that he has been reading repeatedly, he will most likely become confused and end up with a false interpretation of the text, running the risk of losing his grasp on the insight that he now finds so compelling. And so he decides to close the book and to avoid, as much as he can, further thought on the subject for the night. Whenever a thought about the paragraph threatens to enter his mind, he chases it away, and tells himself in a stern inner voice that he has already found the correct interpretation of the text, and that's it. He does *not* do so out of considerations of convenience (unlike Laura, he is not motivated by a desire to finish his work by a certain date). His only concern is to come up with a true interpretation, and he decides to "lock in" his belief in the truth of his interpretation purely because he knows that this belief is more likely to be true and justified than any belief that the might develop later, his mind fuddled by fatigue and by the effects of staring at the same paragraph again and again.

3. *The Epistemic Self-Improvement Project.* Loretta realizes that many of her beliefs have originated in unreliable sources of information. She is not, really, very credulous, but she is likely to forget, for example, that the place in which she read that a woman is more likely to be hit by lightning than to get married after forty was a dubious self-help book that she leafed through at an airport, and therefore is inclined to believe this statement as if she had found it in a more trustworthy document. One day she decides to try to improve her epistemic situation. She avoids reading self-help books and tabloids, and when she hears something that sounds like an interesting fact, she writes it down and tries to find reliable confirmation. Her reasons for the project are not reasons of expedience (she is not trying to avoid social embarrassment, say) or moral reasons (the beliefs in question do not concern her job, for example). She simply sees some value in having a more accurate picture of the world.

4. *Enough is enough*. Paul has discovered a mathematical proof, or so it seems. Again and again he traces his logical steps attempting to make sure that he has made no mistakes. Eventually he says to himself, "Ok, that's it. I have finished." He saves his file, calls one of his friends on the phone, and mentions that he has found the proof. Cautiously, he adds that of course he will double-check his steps again tomorrow morning, just in case. Right now, so soon after he wrote the proof, it is no use checking—he is likely to overlook mistakes.

Wishful thinking. Wishful thinking is nicely exemplified by Sigmund Freud walking down a city street and misreading a storefront sign as saying "Antiquities." This apparently happened to him often, as he was a great lover of antiquities and was enthusiastic about buying and collecting them. Most of the time, he would be disappointed to discover that he was just beholding an ordinary store. But now, in wishful thinking, one is said to believe "what one wants to believe." Once again, though, an examination of this sort of case shows that there is no ground here for believing at will.

As Alfred Mele and Ariela Lazar have argued (Mele 2000; Lazar 1999), cases of wishful thinking such as Freud's are best explained without appeal to voluntary control over belief (see also Arpaly 2002, 11–12). After all, why would Freud *decide* to see antiquities shops where there were none? This habit causes him again and again to approach a building with the hope of finding some historical artifacts for sale and to experience the pain of disappointment, as well as to be inconvenienced in other ways. It is better to think of wishful thinking as part of a larger group of phenomena that can be described (following Lazar 1999) as "belief under the influence" — cases in which emotions skew our belief-forming processes in ways that, although sensitive to what we want, are most definitely *not* reflective of practical rationality. In addition to wishful thinking, there is, for example, fearful thinking (as when you hear steps and you are sure it must be a criminal) and self-hateful thinking (a thin anorectic seeing herself as fat). In the same vein, there is also depressed thinking—Peter Kramer, in *Listening to Prozac*, describes a woman who always believed that her cousin was taller than she was, until she recovered from depression, when she learned that in fact the cousin was the shorter one (Kramer 1993). It is not surprising, in the light of the common occurrence of these things, that wishful thinking exists as well: if self-hatred can make you see yourself as ugly, then self-love might make you see yourself as good looking. If fear might make you likely to think that the steps you hear are those of a criminal, a more optimistic mood might make you likely to think that these are the steps of the nice person for whom you are waiting. There is no reason to assume genuine *choice* in any of these cases: the influence of desire upon belief seems to be below the level of any determination of what would be practically beneficial.

This is not to deny that there also exist cases of deliberate self-deception, but these are cases that involve manipulating or sabotaging one's belief-forming mechanism, as when a person tries to smother a suspicion of marital infidelity by stopping herself from reflecting on the subject, avoiding occasions on which she is likely to find evidence, telling herself "it is going to be okay," and so forth. In such a case, as in the others, there is no need to posit the ability to control beliefs the way we control arm movements.

BELIEF, CHOICE, AND RESPONDING TO EPISTEMIC REASONS

So far, I have relied on fairly particular considerations in arguing that 'ought' does not imply 'can'. Evidence from the ordinary experience of having beliefs and from the details of particular cases in which we might be tempted to say that a person chose to believe have so far suggested that epistemic norms do not come with corresponding abilities to *act* so as to meet the norms. In arguing that responding to epistemic reasons is not a matter of choice, I do not wish to rely on everyday phenomenology overmuch, however. As I have pointed out, there are many cases in which people who do not have the *experience* of AR freedom nonetheless act as freely as anyone ever does. If so, then the lack of felt freedom over belief should not be relied on as evidence that we have no such freedom, and the apparent absence of freedom in cases of so-called choosing to believe cases might still be compatible with the presence of genuine freedom. This section will take a different approach. Doing what one wants usually sounds like a good thing. On the other hand, believing what one wants to believe usually sounds like a state in which something is epistemologically amiss. The gap between these two facts will be used to argue, this time on fairly general grounds, that epistemic 'ought's do not require anything like epistemic freedom.

It should not be said that it is never desirable to believe what one wants to believe—there are situations in which it might be a good idea—but the fact that I want to believe P is never by itself an *epistemic* reason to believe P. If you ask me, "Why do you believe that the Marianna Trench is near Guam?" and I answer, "Because I want to believe it," you might think that I have a practical reason to believe that the Marianna Trench is near Guam, but you have no reason yet to think I have the least epistemic justification for my belief. In general, practical reasons for belief are not epistemic reasons.

A duty epistemologist might point out that people do not always chose to believe things "just because you want to." If we are dutiful or virtuous or conscientious, what we want to do is the right epistemic thing—believe something that is true, or justified, or likely, for example (e.g., Steup 2001). Like the moral agent who wants to do the right thing, the ideal epistemic agent will always defer to epistemic reasons rather than to other practical reasons to believe.

The duty epistemologist's picture is misguided, however. In order to decide to believe something because it is true, justified, or likely, one must already have a belief about its truth, justification, or likelihood. Suppose I am trying to find out if Jung was an anti-Semite, the question being raised for me. I pore over relevant books, transcripts of his interviews, biographies, memoirs and such. I pore over the published arguments made by historians for and against. Perhaps I want to believe that he was not an anti-Semite, but I also have a commitment to searching for the truth. After I finish doing my reading, I conclude that yes, he was an anti-Semite, based on imperfect but not insubstantial evidence of the sort one relies on in answering such questions.

Now suppose that I *decide* to believe that Jung was an anti-Semite. I decide to believe it not simply in the sense that, satisfied that I have done my research well, I decide to leave my desk, have some coffee, and make it psychologically unlikely that I'll doubt my conclusion in the absence of new evidence. This, as suggested above, would be deciding to manipulate my belief-forming mechanism, but here we want to assume that I actually decide to *believe* that Jung was an anti-Semite, that the decision plays a direct role in forming the belief.

So, why did I decide to believe Jung was an anti-Semite? If I am epistemically vicious, I might have decided it just because I wanted to, or because I am already ill-disposed toward Jung on other grounds, or the like. None of these would be good epistemic reasons, of course. But suppose I have been epistemically dutiful: I decide to believe that Jung was an anti-Semite because it is the truth (perhaps, the deontic epistemologist might add, I have even done so against the temptation to believe "what I wanted to believe" instead). But of course, the mere fact of Jung's anti-Semitism (assuming it is a fact) cannot cause my decision directly: it needs to be mediated by my belief that it is a fact. So if I am epistemically virtuous, then I decide to believe that Jung was an anti-Semite because I believe it to be a fact that Jung was an anti-Semite. Instead of deciding to believe Q for epistemically vicious reasons, I decide to believe P because I believe P to be true, and want to believe the truth. But of course, the decision is then redundant: it comes after I already believe that P.

Now perhaps it is not exactly truth that we are committed to when we are epistemically virtuous, but a more complex standard. For example, perhaps an epistemically dutiful person is bound to believe what the evidence suggests. So perhaps my reasoning went this way: I believed that the evidence suggests that Jung was an anti-Semite, and, being epistemically dutiful, I wanted to believe what the evidence suggests, and because of that decided to believe that Jung was an anti-Semite. But again it can be asked, why do I want to believe what the evidence suggests? Again, one possible answer is "simply because I wanted to," which is not a good epistemic reason. The obvious alternative is "I wanted to believe what the evidence suggests, I believed that the evidence suggests that Jung was an anti-Semite, and therefore I decided to believe that Jung was an anti-Semite." Here again we run into a dilemma: either I believe what the evidence suggests for vicious reasons or I believe what the evidence suggests because I believe that the evidence suggests it—an explanation that makes the question of what I wanted to believe irrelevant. However we define our standard of epistemic justification—that which is true, that which the evidence suggests, that which is more than 50 percent likely to be true, or what have you—at some point we hit rock bottom, a point at which either one has a belief that is not epistemically rational or one's adherence to the epistemic standard is not a matter of decision.

Thus, if my belief that Jung was an anti-Semite was a good response to an epistemic reason, it could not have been a "decision." And if a proper response to epistemic reasons is not a decision, failing to respond to it is not a decision either. Looking at the evidence, I either "get it"—respond to the relevant reasons—or I do not. I do not go through a decision process (which in any case would be a curious process if, for example, it could lead to deciding to make such mistakes as deducing "Homer lived in the first century" from "Homer was the first Greek poet" during an exam). Even if something like love or hatred for Jung ruins my objectivity and, unbeknownst to me, clouds my perception of the evidence in front of my eyes, what it does is prevent me from seeing what the evidence suggests. Of course, there are also cases in which a belief has already formed in me in response to the evidence, but I hate it so much that I start manipulating my belief-forming apparatus so as to bury it or get rid of it if I can. This would be a case in which I make myself epistemically irrational—whether for bad practical reasons or, at times, for good ones.

Does this mean that there is no legitimate way to talk about epistemic duties? As we have seen, there might be things that one would be required to do if one wants to be a good epistemic agent—things that are practically required of anyone whose goal is to be a good theoretician (whether out of love for the truth or because it makes it possible to be a morally better person or because it helps one to be prudent). Whatever reason one has to want to be a good belief-former, some actions might be helpful or required: drinking coffee, avoiding tabloids, taking critical thinking classes, or making it a point to "do one's homework" —to seek as much information as one can to make it likely that one's reasoning or reflection will conduce to the truth. One might wish to call these things "epistemic duties," but they are not duties to *believe*. If my student, after taking a course in critical thinking, drinking coffee, rereading her lecture notes, and otherwise doing all in her power to improve her mind, commits outrageous fallacies with the same frequency as before all her efforts, she will be just as epistemically irrational, or even more epistemically irrational, than before, however impressive her commitment to the above "duties." She would be a person who tried to make herself epistemically rational and failed, while her fellow student, who never made the slightest effort to better herself, might still be more rational than she is. This is why I prefer to think of pure epistemic norms—such as the norm that says that one should not believe a contradiction—as norms or 'oughts' rather than duties. In true deontology, As are given for effort.

While I reject epistemic duties (properly so called), my view does allow for epistemic *virtues*. Even though we do not choose to believe things, what we care about influences what we believe, or even what we perceive, and if we are deeply concerned with truth or theoretical justification, we are considerably less susceptible than others to some types of motivated epistemic irrationality. What we care about influences our deliberation, perception, and other cognitive processes. If you care passionately about being at work on time, you are less likely to underestimate the amount of time you need to get to work, all else being equal, than someone who does not care as much. If you love a woman then, all else being equal, you remember your dates with her better than you would otherwise: not because you make a point of writing them down clearly or memorizing them, but because you don't need to, because you remember them as a direct result of your love. If you do not care much for math, but care a lot about your finances, chances are that you are better able to solve arithmetic problems that involve your money than those that do not, even when the problems differ only in abstractness of presentation. And so on. Such familiar patterns repeat when people are motivated to be irrational, too. If two people are comparably motivated to hide from certain facts they believe to hold, but one person cares more about the truth, then the latter person will be less likely to form a motivated irrational belief than the former—again, all else being equal.

Here is a nice, illustrative case.[5] A guest on a talk show tells us a story of how it dawned on her that Jesus exists, saying, "I was all alone in a foreign country. I was sad because my father had recently died. I tried several times to get a job as an actress, and failed. Then I discovered that one of my last boyfriends had AIDS. That was the worst moment of these dreadful two weeks. I was due for another audition the next day, and I didn't know how I could concentrate. I felt completely alone, and it scared me. Suddenly, when I was in bed, trying to sleep, it dawned on me that I can't really be so alone. It is simply impossible for life to be so unbearable; someone must be watching me. Jesus must be watching me. I felt an immense relief and found myself calm enough the next day to audition successfully." The inference from the fact that one had two horrible weeks to the existence of Jesus is not a good one, and from the way the talk-show guest describes the process she has undergone, one gets a distinct impression of wishful thinking—dramatic, desperate wishful thinking.

A person whose concern for truth and reason is so deep that placed in comparable circumstances, these concerns prevent such wishful thinking can be said to be epistemically virtuous. Compare the reaction of the talk-show guest to the reactions of another person. Lance Armstrong, having survived an advanced case of cancer against long odds, explains in his autobiographical books (2001, 2003) that it never seriously occurred to him to think that he "beat" cancer in a "brave" battle—luck played a large role in his survival, he explains, and so did the expertise of the first-rate doctors who helped him. A person famous for his fierce willpower, Armstrong shrugs away the idea that attitude beats cancer: he reminds us that people with great attitudes have died and people with poor attitudes have resumed their ornery lives. He also explains, in a similar manner, that he sees no reason to conclude from his survival that God exists. Especially given the

---

[5] First discussed in Arpaly 2003, 56.

fact that Armstrong is not an intellectual and not particularly well-educated, what he seems to demonstrate here is an epistemic virtue: a concern for truth, honesty, and accuracy that made him immune, in the case described, to the sort of wishful thinking that happened to the talk-show guest and which would probably happen to many of us if we were to experience such a harrowing tale as Armstrong's. It is not credible to imagine that the talk-show guest and Armstrong both felt the pull of logic and the pull of wishful thinking and then decided between them. I would not be surprised, however, if it is the case is that one of them had more concern for truth and epistemic justification than the other. The difference between them would then be not in adherence or nonadherence to an epistemic duty but in the possession or absence of a virtue.

The Case of Moral Ought

To recapitulate: There are genuine epistemic norms: people who infer from P and P → Q and the absence of strong evidence that not Q to the conclusion that Q come to believe what they *ought* to believe in such circumstances, and are thereby epistemically rational; to have believed otherwise would have been to have believed something irrational, to have believed something they *ought not* to have believed. In spite of these normative truths, however, there are no corresponding epistemic abilities. People lack the ability to decide or choose what to believe, and so a fortiori lack the ability to decide or choose to believe what they ought to believe. Nonetheless, they ought to believe it. 'Ought', then, does not imply 'can' in the strong sense relevant to a debate between compatibilists and incompatibilists, the sense in which an obligation requires a power to bring it about that the obligation is fulfilled. Epistemic 'ought' implies epistemic 'can' in at most the weak sense that for it to be true that one ought to believe that P, one must have the conceptual resources necessary to formulate the thought that P: P must be the sort of thing that, if it occurred to one with sufficient force, one might come to believe it. This being the case, I see no reason to conclude from general principles that practical 'oughts' imply practical 'cans' in any more dramatic sense. 'Ought' does not *in general* imply 'can'.

So 'ought' does not in principle imply 'can'—not even the kind of 'ought' that provides reasons and implies judgments about rationality. But what if there is something special about *moral* 'ought'?

One gut intuition can be expressed in the words that morality, unlike epistemic norms and other norms, needs to be *fair*. Put in these words, this claim strikes me as unclear. Fairness is part of morality, and so to talk of morality being fair is like talking about morality being moral (or aesthetics being beautiful, say). If morality is fair, does it mean that I can say, "Look, morality, I have done three superarrogatory acts last week. Surely I can get away with lying to a student today." This is where Anscombe would probably suspect us of being under the spell of regarding morality as a set of commands from a celestial boss, who can be fair or unfair to us.

Then, of course, there are examples involving terrestrial bosses. David Copp (1995) reminds us that one is unfair if one, say, orders an employee to do something impossible—fly, for example. The fact that the employee can't fly seems by itself to be sufficient for the conclusion that it is not true that she ought to fly. But one could explain the unfairness of this case by appealing not to the fact that the employee, in some modal sense, cannot fly, but to the fact that, what with her lack of wings, she cannot make herself fly simply by wanting and/or intending to do so.. Something like "Ought implies can-bring-about-by-wanting" seems to explain all the standard, non-controversial cases in which a requirement is regarded as unfair because of an inability: hence the excuse "due to circumstances that are not under my control."[6]

More compellingly, Copp argues that morality is *action guiding*, that it is meant to guide us in deliberation, and that when one deliberates what to do, there is no point, as it were, in having a principle that tells you to do something that you cannot do. To those who, like me, want to replace "cannot bring about by wanting" for "cannot do," Copp provides the following counter-example:

Madeleine considers whether or not to lie for reasons of convenience. Unbeknownst to her, an Evil Count has the ability to read and control her mind. If he predicts that she may develop a desire to tell the truth, the count will immediately make it the case that she has a desire to lie, and thus make sure that she lies anyway. Madeleine does lie, without any intervention from the count. Is it true of her that she ought not to have lied? Note that in this story, telling the truth is not something that the agent can bring about by willing.[7]

---

[6] See Sinnot-Armstrong 1984 for a defense of the stronger claim that "ought implies can" is not a claim about real logical implication but a sort of ordinary language implicature.

[7] This example is of course modeled after Frankfurt (1969), with whom Copp disagrees.

This example is just as likely to invoke anti-Copp intuitions as pro-Copp intuitions, but Copp reminds us of the "pointlessness" intuition that he invoked earlier. What good is the maxim "though shalt not lie" for a person in Madeleine's situation? If it cannot guide her through deliberation, what point is there in saying that she ought not to lie?

But a guideline is not pointless just because—*due to circumstances of which we are not aware*—it requires us to do something which, unbeknownst to us, we cannot do. There is nothing wrong with my practical deliberation telling me to take the ten o'clock train on Tuesday just because unbeknownst to me, train workers are currently planning a Tuesday strike. Since Madeleine does not know that there is an Evil Count lurking in the wings, "you ought not to lie" is a good principle for her to consider while deliberating. Naturally, had she been aware of the existence of the Count, it may have been legitimate for her to reach such a practical conclusion as "since the Count is going to manipulate me anyway, I might as well lie without exposing myself to creepy interventions from Evil Counts."

I would like to add the following overlooked truth: while morality is directly action guiding (and, in this way, different from normative epistemology), it is not *merely* action guiding. It is equally action assessing: in fact, when we talk about morality in ordinary life, we often do so not in the context of guiding our own action, but in the context of assessing the actions of others and of past selves ("Do you think he is being a jerk? How could she do this?" Etc.). Morality is also about action assessment, and action assessment, as Kant pointed out, is to a large extent the assessment of the *will* behind the action. We get moral credits for being moved by duty, even though we do not choose to be moved by duty—we only choose to follow it. Will is something that chooses, but it is not, even experientially, something that we choose, just like we cannot choose our beliefs. In that way, morality and normative epistemology are a lot more similar than it seems.

The Science Fiction of Mind Design

Imagine this: one morning, you read in the paper that new technologies have been developed that would give an expert user the ability to change people's brain states by the flick of a switch, to the point of giving them precisely the beliefs or desires one wants to give them. Naturally, the availability of the new technology is worrisome. The government intends to ban it, which will limit the damage somewhat, but there seems to be no way to prevent criminal misuse of the technology. In fact, there has already been a case or two in which the technology has been used. Perhaps there was a case in which a nefarious scientist somehow changed the brain of an innocent person in order to turn him into a willing murderer and then allowed her to revert to her previous benign personality. Perhaps there was a case in which a person was made evil—and remained so. Perhaps there was a case in which a politician's views were irrevocably reversed (and now she does not want them to change back, because naturally she takes them to be true). We can imagine many other baffling cases. Ethical questions immediately arise: What are we to think of such cases? Naturally, the president assembles a committee of top-notch medical ethicists, legal philosophers, psychiatrists, and neurologists to try to figure out what our attitudes to such cases should be and what laws and other social arrangements we should create to accommodate them. The experts are distressed, because they know that the world is about to change, or has changed, irrevocably: a world in which such control of one person's over another's mind is so easily achieved would be very different from the world we know. This change is, perhaps, larger than the one brought about by the introduction of the automobile, the computer, or contemporary reproductive technologies. As practical ethicists do when new technologies arrive, the experts now clutch at what intuition, practice, and old wisdom have told us about more familiar cases, and scramble to derive from these sources some insights that would help us to judge cases involving people who are under the influence of the new technology. They know that their task is going to be hard. They can only hope—desperately—that after they find provisional solutions to the urgent issues, and after enough time passes with the new technology available, and people get a better visceral sense of what living with it is like, commonsense morality will come closer to "wrapping itself around" the radically new possibility.

Thankfully, as of this writing, no such technologies are available. But in philosophy, eminent writers on free will would like us to do, in a way, the reverse of what the experts in my scenario attempt to do: to take cases that would happen in the hypothetical Brave New World under discussion, see whatever intuitions we can muster about them, and apply the resulting insight to real world cases. Hard cases, they say, make bad law, and very artificial cases make problematic sources of intuition.

I shall consider a scenario "artificial" to the extent that it is so different from contemporary, ordinary human experience that if cases of its kind *were* to become part of human experience, the world as a whole would change dramatically. The point is not so much that they are unlikely to ever occur—it is hard to judge how likely anything is—but that it is hard to have any firm opinion as to what would happen should they occur with any regularity. For example, I take Thomson's (1971) scenario in which people grow out of seeds that float in the wind to be very artificial not simply because it is unlikely to occur, but because it is impossible to seriously imagine a world that is "just like ours" except for one little detail—people grow out of seeds that float in the wind. If the structure of reproduction and parenthood were to change so drastically, many other things would change equally drastically, and some of the changes would depend on endless nuances of the imagined situation (Is the process of the growth of humans out of seeds painless to the "farmer"? Does growing them take a lot of work or money? Is there anything that marks a child as "one's own" in the way that DNA does in our world? Do seeds die if one does not plant them? Etc.). I do not wish to argue that very artificial examples cannot be put to good use, but I take it that they should be used with caution.

Philosophical examples of belief and desire induction tend to be artificial. They are very different from, say, hypnosis as used today. Hypnosis, as far as it is understood at all, does not seem to be the straightforward method of *desire induction* that philosophers imagine it to be. Sometimes, it seems to be more similar to one of its more popular images—a method for causing the hypnotic subject to find herself performing certain actions despite not having desires to do them, because the hypnotist has found a way to command the person's body while bypassing the usual channels of desire. At other times, it resembles yet another popular image: the hypnotist inducing an association in the mind of the subject—say, between pizza and worms—which results, unsurprisingly, in the agent forming a desire (say, to avoid pizza). Another thing hypnosis, like sleepiness, may do is loosen a person's inhibitions or weaken her ability to reason, thus making it easier to encourage her to perform certain actions given desires that she already has. This sort of situation, unlike the monstrous desire induction of philosophical science fiction, is not very different from other deviant mental conditions that are not human made, conditions in which standard assumptions about the kind and depth of motivation needed to motivate an action no longer apply. The excuses we make for the hypnotized subject may very well be based, like the excuses given to other deviant people, on the feeling that he is not, after all, acting on a bad desire or at least that he is not acting on a strong bad desire.

We shall now turn to the infamous Dr. Nefarious, who can change desires and beliefs to order, and who can so rather quickly (which enables him, for example, to change your decision at the very moment it is conceived). In my previous book, I conjured Dr. Nefarious inducing in Hapless Patient a desire to kill the Canadian Minister of Sports and Recreation and thus causing him to commit the murder in question. Cases involving Dr. Nefarious have routinely been used in order to show that compatibilist views such as mine, that do not give much thought to the history through which agents have reached their beliefs and desires, must be false. "What if the evil person's evil will have been installed in him by a Dr. Nefarious? Surely you cannot say he is blameworthy, however real his ill will happens to be!" This is how the objection usually goes. In order to answer my philosophical opponents in this matter, I first need to pry away some intuitions invoked by Dr. Nefarious cases that contribute to the confusion they cause.

Consider the following cases:

1. Studies show that the drinking water in the Slippery Rock area contains deposits of lithium. As a result, the residents of the Slippery Rock area tend to be calm and to have a peaceful view of the world.

2. The police discovered that someone from a peace movement has been sneaking lithium into the drinking water of the Slippery Rock area with an eye to inducing a peaceful view of the world in its residents.

3. John is trying to decide what car to buy. The rational choice for him would be a Honda, but he is distracted by images in his head of the nice Mazda his brother has, and irrationally he decides to buy a Mazda instead.

4. John is trying to decide what car to buy. The rational choice for him would be a Honda, but he is distracted by images in his head of a nice Mazda, an image subtly projected into his mind by a psychologically savvy salesman. Irrationally, he decides to buy a Mazda instead.

5. After seven days trapped in a desert cave, thirsty and cold to the point of delirium, I had an epiphany and I became a theist.

6. A clever cult leader, wanting me to become a theist, made sure I was trapped in a desert cave. Having an unusual intuition for such things, he achieved his goal and I became a theist.

7. Due to an inexplicable, arational process, Jay, who did not want a baby, suddenly found himself loving his baby the moment he first laid eyes on her.

8. Due to something his cunning girlfriend put in his drink, Jay, who did not want a baby, suddenly found himself loving his baby as soon as he laid his eyes on her.

All of these agents come to believe or desire some things due to irrational or even arational factors. This is not rare: how many times do people explain changes in their view of the world with observations like "I just got older"? Was the desire to have sex not acquired in the most arbitrary way possible? Those theorists who, like Mele and like Fisher, put particular importance on the history through which we have reached our desires, values, and beliefs need to take into account that even in the most normal lives or the lives of the most reasoning and reflective people, this history is checkered. But there is something important to notice here.

Our gut reaction to the stories above is very different when these changes occur "naturally" and when these changes occur as a result of the deliberate action of a fellow human. We greatly fear being under the control of another human—even in circumstances where being under the control of "hormones," "something in the air," evolution, our own irrationality, and many other things would not bother us. But it must be noted that whatever it is that makes us fear the possibility of a mental change induced by a sneaky human more than the possibility of the same change induced, equally sneakily, by some force of nature has *nothing to do with moral responsibility*. Why would a person who is acting under the influence of a chemical that someone intentionally sneaked into his water be less (or more) morally responsible than someone who drank water which, unbeknownst to him, contains that chemical naturally? If Jay changes as a result of a hormone in his body, what difference does it make, when it comes to moral responsibility, whether the hormonal change, which is not a particularly unusual one, naturally occurred or whether the person's partner secretly injected him with some? We obviously have a strong aversion to being manipulated by others, and this observation may be of great interest to value theory. As far as moral responsibility goes, though, it is hard to see how being shaped by the gloomy weather in your town is somehow different from being shaped by the manipulations of a fellow human being. Thus, one type of deep fear invoked by the Dr. Nefarious scenarios, although compelling, must not have too much influence on us when we try to develop a view as to the moral blameworthiness of Dr. Nefarious's victims.

Let us return to our sample scenario. Dr. Nefarious changed the brain of her Hapless Patient so that he will murder the Canadian Minister of Sports and Recreation. What, then, of the moral worth of HP's actions? One scenario I would like to discuss only briefly: the scenario in which HP is already a fairly murderous type, and all Dr. Nefarious had to do was to tip him toward killing the Minister, the way that something I heard on the bus today or the cheerful look of the weather may tip me, in a whimsical kind of way, to think of a new paper on virtue instead of reworking an old paper on autonomy. This would be a "lithium in the water" case in an almost straightforward way. The interesting case is the case in which out of the blue, a person who may have never even heard about the Minister of Sports and Recreation and who, more importantly, would never ordinarily commit murder or any other severe crime, is suddenly induced by Dr. Nefarious to do just that.

As to this kind of case, I think there are three kinds of scenarios that need discussion. In one sort of scenario, the "Patty Hearst scenario," Dr. Nefarious creates a bad person out of HP, and HP is like a born-again Robert Harris, a "born-again" case of bad constitutive moral luck. In this sort of scenario, HP is fully blameworthy for bad deeds done after Dr. Nefarious's intervention. In other scenarios, Dr. Nefarious creates in HP something similar to a compulsion, or a very unwilling addiction, and HP deserves little or no blame. In yet a third kind of scenario, profound puzzles about personal identity may have to be solved before any proper assignment of blame or innocence can be made.

How does Dr. Nefarious make HP commit the murder? The standard story is that she instills an irresistible desire in him. But desires are only irresistible or resistible given the motivational structure of the specific agent involved. For most people under most circumstances, the desire to avoid death is quite close to irresistible, and still this desire is resistible to a devoted soldier, a suicide bomber, a person extremely attracted to danger, or a very sad person. For many people, the desire to chat on the Internet is relatively easy to resist, but to a person who is extremely lonely, chatting on the Internet can become so irresistible that it can become something very similar to frightening physical addiction, and just as destructive. Heroin addiction is very powerful, but people have succeeded in quitting, and there are even a few rare reports of people who managed to be "moderate heroin users." A universally irresistible desire would be a desire that is

irresistible within any human motivational structure under all circumstances. Presumably, the desire to avoid some extreme forms of torture is
such a desire, but I suspect few others are. Usually, when we talk about
irresistible desires, the irresistibility is of some more qualified kind.

So Dr. Nefarious, in order to make HP commit the murder, not only
has to instill a desire in HP to kill the Canadian Minister of Sports and
Recreation, but she also has to make the desire irresistible to him. Many
of the methods available to her are ones that involve *turning HP into a*
murderer (albeit a strange one). For example, Dr. Nefarious may instill in
HP an intrinsic desire to kill the Canadian Minister that is much stronger
then all his other desires, and in that way irresistible to him. This would
be turning HP into the equivalent of a person who hates another so much
that he can't stand the thought of his existing, and would—akratically or
otherwise—forfeit the satisfaction of all of his other desires in order to kill
him (a sort of fanatic with a particularly strange cause). Or she may give
him a desire to kill the minister that is fairly strong, but change the rest of
his personality in such a way that the desire would be completely unop-
posed. In both cases, HP currently has the psychology of a bad or blameworthy person, except that he acquired that psychology in a strange way.

If this view sounds strange, consider the case of Patty Hearst—perhaps
as close as reality gets to the story of Dr. Nefarious. Brainwashed by her
captors, albeit by considerably more arduous methods than those Dr. Nefarious seems to use, Hearst joined their terrorist organization and was
eventually convicted for her crimes despite the fact of her nonrational
change in motivations. Note that it matters very little to our judgment
if she has indeed been brainwashed deliberately or if she just converted,
irrationally, due to the duress she was under (the "Stockholm Syndrome").
In either case, a drastic change in her belief-desire set happened irrationally
and rather quickly, and in either case the person who stood before the court
seems to have been a wholehearted terrorist who was blameworthy for her
actions, not an innocent woman acting under great duress. Stress may cause
people to act out of character, but it may also truly *change their characters*,
and this is what seems to have happened in the case of Hearst.

Now, just as in the discussion of HP's *agent autonomy* one is distracted
by the fact that he is dependent on Dr. Nefarious, so in discussing HP's
moral responsibility, one faces the following distracting factor—that Dr.
Nefarious obviously *is* blameworthy for turning HP murderous, and thus
in an indirect way for causing the murder. Similarly, if Hearst's captors
intentionally made a terrorist out of her, they are also blameworthy for
making her so. Dr. Nefarious and the terrorists are analogous in this way

to Robert Harris's parents as discussed in chapter 1. One can also be distracted by the fact that HP's desire to kill the Canadian Minister and Hearst's political convictions were acquired very nonrationally: but then, the desire to have sex is also acquired nonrationally, and people who act on it, if they do something wrong, are still blameworthy. I have argued above that if we treat nonrational personality changes as excluding subsequent autonomy, too few people are autonomous. Similarly, if we exempt from blame any murderer or terrorist whose convictions or character were acquired irrationally, we would exempt too many murderers and terrorists.

But turning HP into a murderer is only one way to give him an irresistible desire to kill the Canadian Minister. Dr. Nefarious might, instead, turn him into a person with a (very) deviant mental condition. She might induce false beliefs in him that would make the murder a reasonable thing to perform—for example, a coherent delusion that the Minister is about to take over Canada and become a dictator. She can craft a nonpsychological, neurological condition in which the thought of not killing the minister will induce very severe physical pain in poor HP—a caricature of drug addiction. In these cases, HP will surely be much less blameworthy, if at all. Or she may turn him into a caricature of an impulse-control disorder. Imagine that you wake one morning with a desire to murder the Canadian Minister of Sports and Recreation, and nothing else has changed in your brain. If you are anything like me, you will find yourself with a desire radically lacking in integration. That is, your desire will be so essentially opposed to the rest of your attitudes, including your deepest ideas and concerns, that it would make the offending desires of the most unwilling heroin addict or kleptomaniac look positively wholehearted. This is the state we often imagine post-operation HP to be in. But how can a desire so ridiculously opposed by any other part of the patient's mind motivate him to murder? Either Dr. Nefarious has made the desire also ridiculously deep, in which case she has turned him into a murderer, after all: or she gave him a neurological impulse control disorder that ruins the ordinary relations between the depth of desire and motivational power, made him an extreme caricature of Tourette's or kleptomania or ADD, a person in whom a desire of ordinary depth results, due to some brain mishap, in a ridiculously strong urge that cannot be subdued even by the fact that the rest of HP's psyche, including his deepest concerns, oppose it. On such a scenario, HP merits very little blame, simply because his action manifests very little ill will or lack of good will.

I have looked at two kinds of scenarios—HP is changed into a murderer or a more sophisticated trick is played upon him[1] But perhaps much of our

---

[1]Another scenario is the one in which HP has always been the murderous type, and all Dr. Nefarious had to do was to add to his mix a specific desire to kill the Canadian Minister. For

tendency to look at HP as exempt from blame comes from our response to a third kind of scenario: the one in which HP is changed into a murderer, *and then changed back*. Imagine that HP, an ordinary person, is changed into a murderer by Dr. Nefarious. After he kills the Canadian Minister, Dr. Nefarious has no use for him, and she allows him to revert to his previous, morally average personality. Later, his lawyer cites Dr. Nefarious's medical operation as his defense. Am I going to argue that no such defense is available to him? No. I am going to argue that this story illustrates yet another thing that makes Dr. Nefarious stories so hard to wrap our intuition around: they involve people undergoing, by the flick of a switch, transformations that in real life occur rarely, and if they do, they occur in twenty or fifty years, not in a moment, and if they happen and then go away, they never leave the person as the same person who existed before them. I tend to think that the defense genuinely available to HP is a very extreme, very decisive, and particularly convincing variant of the defense available to a good person who committed a crime fifty years ago, long before he found Jesus and underwent tremendous positive changes in personality: "My client is a completely different man now." Even such a case is complicated (if he is such a different person, why did he not turn himself in?) but at times we are strongly grabbed by the intuition that it would be futile to disturb a good person who worked hard to compensate for his crime just because of something he did when he was almost a different person. The case of Dr. Nefarious is, of course, more complicated. As we imagine Dr. Nefarious to have unlimited powers to change HP's brain to fit her plans, the case of the changed and re-changed HP raises hard questions of *personal identity* which seldom, if ever, arise in real life. Should we punish Dr. Jekyll for the actions of Mr. Hyde? The question of whether we should blame HP for the actions of the modified HP is the same question, perhaps posed even more sharply, because some of the more romantic interpretations of Stevenson's story are ruled out (that is, HP Hyde did *not* spring out of HP Jekyll's own suppressed desires but was arbitrarily created by Dr. Nefarious). Whether we should blame HP Jekyll for HP Hyde's action is a hard question, and the air surrounding it is not exactly thick with reliable intuitions. I take it that a case involving puzzles about personal identity should not be used as a test case for theories about moral responsibility.

HP's pre-treatment personality to be such that his newly instilled desire would not be fiercely opposed by the rest of him, he needs to be very callous in his attitude toward human life. In this case, his desire to kill the Minister would be like any number of murderous desires which he would develop in response to irrational factors such as anger, stress, or the color of the sky. True, it is a stranger desire than most of these, but this *is* a science-fiction example.

WHEN CHEAP WILL JUST WON'T DO

EVEN IF WE SHARE with rattlesnakes the property of being causally determined, we can still respond to reasons, and so we can still have meaningful lives, subject to moral, epistemic, and other norms. Who can ask for anything more?

Some people do, even granted that reason responsivness and moral praise and blameworthiness exist in a deterministic world. Somehow, the responsibility and reason-responsiveness that I have described here is not enough for them. They want a higher sense of self-authorship, Absolute Responsibility (Kane 1998) or origination (Honderich 2002) or the elusive state described by Paul the Pessimist as the ability to choose what to want. They want a state in which it is true somehow that as a human being you have control over your mental states, as opposed to being made of, or identical to, the sum total of your mental states, some of which could be controlled by others; they want "autonomy," they want "free will." They want these things either *in addition* to things like moral responsibility and meaningful relationships, or as a special addition to things like moral responsibility and meaningful relationships—something that makes them more valuable, more deeply *ours*.

Thomas Nagel thinks that all of us crave such freedom for its own sake—a freedom to choose not only what to do, but who to be: a freedom to treat our own mental states, our "empirical selves," as mere circumstances, and make our decisions—even our decisions *about* our mental states—independently of them (Nagel 1986). We desire, he says, to "intervene with the world"—including our empirical selves—"from outside." Or, barring that:

> I wish to act not only in light of the external circumstances facing me and the possibilities that they leave open, but in light of the internal circumstances as well: my desires, beliefs, feelings, and impulses. I wish to be able to subject my motives, principles, and habits to critical examination, so that nothing moves me to action without my agreeing to it. In a way, the setting against

which I act is gradually enlarged and extended inward, till it includes more
and more of myself, considered as one of the contents of the world. (107)

Some people have the desire for complete self-authorship as described by
Nagel, and some do not. Like people who want to have children finding it
hard to believe that some people do not want children, people who have
the desire for self-authorship find it hard to believe that some of us do not
have a desire for self-authorship. To be more precise, some of us have a
deep craving for self-authorship as described by Nagel, some of us find the
whole idea of self-authorship overrated, and then there are many people
who have some craving for self-authorship but who, upon further ques-
tioning, turn out to crave self-authorship in a much less strict sense than
Nagel's. For example, a person might dislike the thought of having her
way paved for her by a rich father and relish the idea that she has achieved
good things through hard work, enterprise, and talent, but not care very
much whether there is some metaphysical sense in which her talent and
hard-working nature are determined.

This chapter is dedicated to exploring these attitudes. I begin in a contrary spirit, by highlighting cases in which people seem to want the absence
of such self-authorship, or at least want things that are incompatible with
self-authorship:

1. *It's written in the stars.* There are people who are fond of believing in astrology, holding that the courses of their lives are to a large extent dependent
   on things that happen in the sky, over which they have no control. There
   seems to be something about the idea of supernatural laws, as in astrology
   and numerology, that makes them more attractive to some people than
   natural laws: perhaps the difference is that supernatural laws are perceived
   as anthropocentric or teleological, while natural laws are not. But this does
   not change the fact that one does not have any more control over things
   that are "written in the stars" than one has over things that are written in
   a more conventional ways in one's DNA and environment.

2. *Blood, tradition, and identity.* Consider such expressions as "rock and roll is
   in my blood," "Texas born and bred," "it's a guy thing" (or "a girl thing"),
   and "I am my father's son." Some, though by no means all, of the people
   who say these things *relish* saying them, treating as a spoilsport anyone
   who mentions that some rockers, Texans, men, women, and descendents of
   imposing family traditions have chosen to act differently. It seems that, at
   times, people enjoy the idea of having a firm, robust identity, which comes
   more easily if one assumes that belonging to certain groups or types ensures

particular behaviors. As philosophers are often quite individualistic, we can forget that some prefer being a derivative work of art to being an original.

3. *I'm gonna lose control / And I think I like it.* These and other song lyrics suggest a craving for being swept off of one's feet or losing oneself. Sometimes the craving in question is a craving for romantic necessity. At other times, though, one seems to simply crave *abandon*—even the sort that cannot be interpreted as something as lofty as romantic necessity.

4. *Higher powers and going with the flow.* Consider the twelve-step-group member who thinks that salvation comes with abandoning one's will and surrendering to a higher power, or the devout Christian who attributes his sins to "willfulness" and his good behavior to God's grace. Also consider the recovery movement—the phenomenon of people who wish to define as addictions or diseases all kinds of behavior that scientists do not regard as such, especially so they can start twelve-step groups and "give themselves over to a higher power." A milder relative of this view is the idea that one should "go with the flow"—that is, relinquish attempts to control one's life and accept things as they are instead.

One might remark that on some occasions, the wish to be out of control or to believe that one has no choice might stem from a desire to be exempt, in one's own eyes, from moral responsibility. While Luther's "I can do no other" is meant to be an assumption, rather than a rejection, of moral responsibility, it seems clear that sometimes expressions such as "it's a guy thing" and "I am my father's son" are used to evade moral responsibility—in one's own eyes as well as in the eyes of others. This is not always the case, however. The person who sees himself as "Texas born and bred" might see himself that way without any desire to evade moral responsibility, and might even feel proud and praiseworthy for good actions or virtues that are typical of the sort of person he takes himself to be. But more importantly, even cases in which phrases such as "boys will be boys" are used by agents to avoid seeing themselves as morally responsible, their craving has something un-Nagelian about it: it seems as if we do not always desire to be responsible for our actions, and so free will does *not* always seem attractive.

Turn now to those who do not necessarily wish for passivity, but who do not seem to have a particular desire for Nagel agency either—that is, to those who do not have a particular desire for their preferences and traits to have been chosen by them. It is, of course, nearly tautological that we would all prefer to have only those preferences that we prefer or of which we approve, but it does not seem that we are always particular as to whether we have those preferences as a result of choice as opposed to luck or fate. I might want to be beautiful without wanting to have the ability to choose whether to be beautiful or not, and the same might be true of wanting to have certain preferences. Many people feel lucky that they have, say, a certain sexual orientation or that they are Yankees fans, and would not find it distressing to know that their sexual orientations are innate or that their love of the New York Yankees was inevitable given their upbringings. Some people feel lucky in that they are (or are not) ambitious, that they do (or do not) have the desire to have children, that they are (or are not) patriotic, or in love, or concerned with the state of the world—and would not be particularly bothered if they were suddenly to discover that the taste, preference, or concern in question was in fact causally determined, that fate had left no alternative. If a person feels wholeheartedly happy about having, or not having, a certain desire or preference, she might not even particularly mind discovering that the existence or non-existence of said preference or desire is the result of the stealthy actions of a mad scientist or a freak accident involving being struck by lightning when she was three years old.

It might also be possible to be dissatisfied with a preference or a character trait, and wish for a different one, without being particular about the desired change being a result of one's choice. Like Sky Masterson in *Guys and Dolls*, you might want lady luck to be kind to you without particularly wishing not to depend on luck. Or you might wish for a certain preference—wish you could be less clingy, have less of a sadistic streak, have less of a sweet tooth, care less about what people think, or have fewer conflicting desires— but not mind it at all, or even prefer it, that the change in preference would be "natural" ("growing up," say) as opposed to your own doing.

For some people, then, it is good enough if you have what you want and want what you have. The philosophical counterpart for this idea is to be found in the various theories holding that freedom, or something close enough to it, is present when one has the desires one wants to have or has the desires one values or has the preferences one prefers to have. The most famous theory of such sort is that of Harry Frankfurt (1971), according to which you are free if you act on desires that you desire to motivate you.[1] You need to have the will you want, as it were, but it is not necessary that you have the will you want *because* you want it—not even in the limited sense of your second-order desires somehow causing you to act for the right first-order desires. But this, too, is not enough for all of us.

[1] See also; Gerold Dworkin 1970; Wright Neely 1974; Eleonore Stump 1988; Keith Lehrer 1990; and others.

Some of us mind it very much that their desires and preferences might not be their choice, and in a way that makes it clear that what they desire is not simply to *have* different preferences, but to have *a choice* over their preferences. This is most evident when we discuss those who are quite satisfied with their current preferences (or even their current lives), but who still wish they had a choice whether to have them or not. Most of us have had moments in which we did not want, for example, to attend the party on Friday but we very much wanted to be invited, so that our failure to show up at the party would be *by choice*. The natural incompatibilist might feel similarly about her preferences: she might feel that if she had the choice, she would like to be the same person that she is, but still be bothered by the thought of not having a choice. Here is an example:

Avi is a passionate teacher and student of literature. In his teens, Avi's parents made clear that they expected him earn a lot of money as an adult, and his peers pressured him to be what they thought to be "cool," but however much he tried, he could not develop preferences in either direction. As the years passed, he stopped trying, and now he likes himself the way he is, and is quite sure that he would choose his current life over the life of a corporate lawyer or a rock singer. He is glad to know that there exist some people who could have had a lucrative or popular job but who chose to be English teachers, but he knows that he, if he tried, would probably not have made it in such a job. This bothers him. When he talks about it, his friends point out—rightly, as it happens—that the reason he would not make a good corporate lawyer, say, is not that he does not have the intellectual talent, but because his heart would not be in it—because he would not *want* it badly enough. That thought comforts him to some extent, but he still wishes he had the capacity, if he wished, to make himself psychologically compatible with being a corporate lawyer. If he had that choice, he would stay just the way he is, admittedly, but still, he wishes he had the choice.

I have discussed craving for self-authorship and the lack of such craving. Also mentioned were cases in which there exists some craving for self-authorship, but not necessarily for Nagelian self-authorship: a craving that can be satisfied by "self-authorship" in a looser sense that does not require ultimate responsibility or origination. To these people, the idea that one is the result of genes and environment is not too disagreeable—at least it appears to them to not be disagreeable once they remember that:

1. It is very rare for two people to have exactly the same genes and it is never true that two people have exactly the same environment.

2. A very small difference in genetics or environment can have a very large cumulative effect on the life of the resulting person.
3. Rare things (platinum, black tigers, synesthesia) and even unique things (the Grand Canyon, the Great Barrier Reef) are just as much part of nature as ordinary things. While one-offs are less likely to be discussed in textbooks, this does not make them supernatural or unnatural.

Many things can satisfy some people's craving for self-authorship: going from rags to riches through hard work and ingenuity; becoming a good person despite coming from a disreputable or bruising background; being able to make personal decisions without much regard for social convention and trends, and without a particular need to defy conventions or trends; being unusual—"an original" about whom it can be said that "she broke the mold" (note the implication there was still a mold); achieving nontrivial though not necessarily grand goals that one has set for oneself; having "self-discipline"; living according to one's own values; being "self-realized" in some psychotherapeutic sense; having the sort of life described in Kipling's poem *If* or the somewhat less stifling sort invoked by " I did it my way."

Consider more carefully the self-made person. For many of us, a person is "self-made" enough to justify the label if she has become successful through her own efforts, rather than, say, through rich parents, and despite obstacles that would have stopped many other people. To admire such a person or to be proud of such a life story is possible for some of us whether or not we think that the effort in question was the result of innate or otherwise determined intelligence, talent, imaginative capacities, high energy levels, high tolerance for pain, or other psychological traits that, innate or not, appear to be acquired very early in life. One might point out that being self-made is most impressive when it would have seemed unlikely in the first place that the person would have come to have the admirable characteristics that helped her along the way: perhaps she is the only diligent person in a family of layabouts, the only person in a bad family to even develop an initial interest in being a better person, the only person with the presence of mind to dare to rebel against a tyrannical tradition that oppressed many others. But beating the odds in terms of the development of one's personality does not require ultimate responsibility: it just requires some improbable things happening and some unprecedented combination of factors. Improbable, but not necessarily unheard of, because the world is complicated enough to produce an infinite number of unique causal circumstances, and because the factors that determine what sort of person one is to become are too numerous to count. Small twists of fate and small genetic differences can have far-reaching consequences. A wealthy person I know who is very proud of "starting from scratch" also says that whatever other factors contributed to the development of hard-working ambition in him, he "could not have done it" without an eccentric uncle who occasionally talked to him when he was a boy, expressing confidence in him and giving idiosyncratic advice that somehow happened to strike a chord when other people's advice had failed to do so. A successful intellectual I know was born to a blue collar family afflicted with domestic violence and has many siblings, none of whom is either successful or intellectually inclined. He told me that he suspects that the course of his life was changed by the fact that he was born with a very large head, making his mother decide that he must be smart and treat him accordingly—that along with a few other factors that are also too idiosyncratic to be discussed in sociology and psychology books. Anyone who has read a good biography or a good Bildungsroman knows that causal explanations of how a person came to be the way she is do not have to be generic explanations ("he was a young man in the period between the two wars," "he was a seventeenth-century philosopher," "she came from a middle class household") or demeaning, reductive ones ("it was all because of his Oedipal complex," "her life has been a long attempt to prove her parents wrong").

What is true of the quality of being self-made is also true of individuality, originality, and creativity, and for similar reasons. To some, there is nothing particularly insulting in comparing a creative genius or an impressively individual personality to a rare bird or a gem or a "sacred monster"— though of course the properties that make the genius unique are different, and generally involve things like content efficacy and reason responsiveness (in addition, sometimes, to atavistic factors such as Maria Callas's voice or Nabokov's incredible memory). To some, the fact that all people are the result of genetic and environmental factors threatens their individuality no more than the individual merits of various cathedrals are threatened by the fact that they are all, after all, made of stone, no more than the fact that a diamond is made of carbon threatens to make it no better than a lump of coal. The very fact that no two people are the same, bodily or mentally, is wrapped in wonder, the very fact that different zygotes make different people is a miracle, and the truth of determinism is not going to change that fact.

Suppose, now, that Paul the Pessimist is a free-will gourmet. He is convinced that only Nagel-type freedom will do and that less radical things, such as being self-made, original, creative, self-realized, living according to one's own values, and so on are merely cheap substitutes for the real thing. On the other hand, Olga the Optimist thinks that there is no particular reason to desire Nagel-type freedom. She regards herself as free enough if she manages to live by her unique set of values, and due to the sort of perspective described above, it does not matter to her if that set of values was determined. How does one adjudicate between them? How does one show that Paul is greedy and whiny, or that Olga has a case of sour grapes or does not understand something important about the human condition? How does one adjudicate a debate as to how much and what kind of free will is worth wanting?

In previous chapters, I have argued that even if determinism is true, we can still have content efficacy and reason responsiveness, and therefore, we can still have moral responsibility as well. Imagine that Paul the Pessimist becomes convinced that I am right in arguing this, but still finds the idea of determinism being true somewhat disturbing. Even while he concedes that being subject to the laws of nature does not deprive him of love, knowledge, meaning, or virtue, he still feels himself somehow constrained by the laws of nature. Does Paul's discomfort make sense? If one has the ability to respond to reasons, with the attendant privileges such as meaning and virtue, but still craves a kind of freedom and feels deprived of it, does it make any sense at all? I would like to argue that yes, it does make sense. It might be "asking too much," a wish for the impossible, but it is nothing like Anscombe's example of wanting to drink a saucer of mud (1969, 70–71).

Look at cases of romantic necessity—cases in which a person "can do no other" because of her values or the power of reasons that she has or both. Harry Frankfurt presents us with one type of such cases, which he calls cases of "volitional necessity." Cases of volitional necessity are cases in which one is compelled to do or not to do something because of what one cares about. Frankfurt's example (1988) is the character Lord Fawn, who suspects that his fiancée has been unfaithful to him and is tempted to spy on her, but quickly finds himself unable to do such a sneaky, ungentlemanly thing because he cares about the values that rule out such behavior. Frankfurt seems to think that Fawn acts freely or autonomously in this case. After all, what can be more free than acting out of one's own deepest values? The idea that being a slave to one's own deepest values, the values that, in a way, make one who one is, is a kind of freedom that has a certain romantic appeal. However, some pessimists are not satisfied with it. They want *real* freedom. But here Frankfurt could ask what more freedom is needed if your actions are an expression of your own values? Given the views I have defended, I can ask the same question, with a slight twist: What more freedom do you need if your actions are an expression of your own value and can also be rational or respond to good reasons?

One reason to doubt that volitional necessity or romantic necessity is freedom is the fact that it does not feel like freedom to the agent. Freedom, by default, is pre-theoretically conceived as what I have been calling 'arm raising freedom'—what I, rightly or wrongly, take myself to have when I say "I can either raise my arm or not, depending on what I want to do." But Frankfurt makes it clear that romantic necessity often feels nothing like AR freedom. Perhaps extremely, completely whole hearted romantic necessity would feel like that: if, out of purity of heart, it never even *occurred* to Fawn to spy on his fiancée, he would not have a chance to feel constrained from doing it. But it does occur to Fawn to spy on his fiancée, and thus he gets the chance to discover that he "just can't do it." Here, the Frankfurtian term *unthinkable* is somewhat misleading. Frankfurt presents Fawn as a person for whom spying on his fiancée is "unthinkable." But perhaps it would be more accurate to say that spying on his fiancée is something that he can think of doing—just not do it or consider it without feeling repelled. Volitional necessities are often discovered through an occasion of temptation or even a resolution to do what the volitional necessity forbids. Fawn is tempted to spy on his fiancée, and he even goes as far as planning to do it: only at that point does he discover that he cannot do it. Even after he discovers that he cannot possibly do so and is disposed never to consider it seriously ever again, we can still imagine him thinking, when his curiosity about his fiancée's doings and his anger at her burn again, such things as "If I were not such a gentleman, I would have caught her by now." This need not make his action less unthinkable to him in Frankfurt's sense. After all, it is still true that Fawn will never be able to bring himself to spy on his fiancée, that he cannot do these things because he cares about certain gentlemanly values, and that he also cares about caring about them—that is, he values being a person with those values.

Similarly, "Here I stand, I can do no other" could easily be the declaration of someone who has often struggled with the temptation to "do other" or with a resolution to be a reasonable, prudent person and to "do other." In fact, even while Luther stands and makes his declaration, having already decided, and, let us assume, having already become disposed, never to consider the possibility of "doing other" seriously ever again, we can imagine him thinking wistfully, in an idle way, of the nice and quiet things he would be doing in his hometown right now if he were not "chosen by God," or by volitional necessity, to see what he saw. To borrow from *Fiddler on the*

Roof, one can feel chosen by God and yet cry, "God! Can't you for once choose someone else?" Again, this would not make it any less true that Luther's faithfulness to his mission is a matter of deep values, and deeply valuing those deep values. If Frankfurt were to require the absence of such wistful thoughts as a necessary condition for volitional necessity, which he does not, there would be very, very little volitional necessity in the world, and it would not be the central phenomenon he takes it to be.

One might not only entertain idle fantasies about being freed from one's volitional necessity but downright rail against it while leaving it in place. A type of action being "unthinkable" for an agent is a matter of the agent's deep concerns, and so is, presumably, an enduring state. A person's concerns, though, are not always evident in her feelings and urges at a given moment: Andrea might love a man so much that harming or leaving him is out of the question for her, and still feel enraged at him rather often. Jean might value her job to the extent that leaving it is something she cannot even consider considering, but she might still often rail against the long hours, the small material rewards, and the very fact that her values and beliefs are such that she would never quit her job, never even take these great vacations that less principled people seem to enjoy. Laurie might break up with her boyfriend because she values religion in a way that he does not, endorse her decision, and all the same wish it didn't matter so much to her.

When we rail against a romantic necessity, what do we want? What would it take for Luther to be in a state in which he "could do other"? What we wish for appears to be the very thing that our incompatibilist, Paul the Pessimist, wants to have: control over one's own mental states. We want a self apart from our mental states that can choose them at will. We want freedom.

If we are to accept Frankfurt's claim that our deep concerns define who we are, and if we assume that Luther's religious values (including, as it were, the values that he values) have such a power over him not because of some akrasia or compulsion but because he cares about them, it seems to be the case that for him to be in a state in which he "could do other" would take such an overhaul of his beliefs, desires, and so forth, that for him to wish for such a state is essentially to wish he were someone else, a logically dubious wish. Even if one rejects strictly Frankfurtian talk of personal identity, one can say that for a tormented artist who embraces his tormented condition to wish he was not a person who would rather endure misery and be creative than forgo misery and not be creative is for him to wish to have a considerable choice as to what sort of person to be. In order to be able to overhaul such a basic thing about himself, he would need to be able to choose lots of beliefs, desires, preferences, and so on. This raises the question of exactly who would be doing the choosing in such a case. It cannot be the combined effect of all of the artist's beliefs, desires, preferences, and other mental states, because ex hypothesi his pro-art attitudes have more sway than his pro-happiness attitudes: this is exactly the situation he wishes he could choose to change. But isn't the artist the same as his collection of attitudes?[2] It seems that in order for the choice to get rid of the volitional necessity to be possible, there would need to be an artist outside of this collection who can modify it if he so wishes. Such absolute self-authorship is, it seems to me, an incoherent notion. If it were possible, Sartre would have been right that human beings are beings who have no nature or essence, and therefore eternally choose who to be.

Or course, libertarians (Clarke 2003; O'Connor 2000; Kane 1998; Ginets 1990; etc.) would argue that such "freedom as to who to be" or something similar enough is a coherent notion, and that we have it: but my goal here is not to argue for or against the libertarians. The question I would like to pose is this: *Suppose* freedom as to who to be is an incoherent notion. Can we still legitimately wish for it? Can we really wish for something incoherent?[3] We do sometimes seem to, at least on the surface, express logically dubious wishes, or at least feel regret that something logically impossible is not the case. I can easily imagine Pythagoras wishing bitterly that the square root of two were a rational number. After all, the discovery that it isn't pained him to a great degree, and he saw it as a serious blow to his theory. We do say things like "I wish I had been Bertrand Russell," and if someone says to us, "Look, if you had been Bertrand Russell, *you* would not have been Bertrand Russell," the pedantic remark does not make us change our wish, but rather regret that it is impossible to fulfill. Many philosophers believe that altering the past through time travel is profoundly incoherent, but if you are a historian trying to figure things out about the scantily documented personal life of Benedictus Spinoza, and in your frustration you say that you wish you could travel to the seventeenth century and do some interviewing, even these philosophers are likely to

---

[2] Of course, there is a complex literature on personal identity which is applicable here. It will be obvious to the reader that I side with the likes of John Locke (1690) and Derek Parfit (1971) against the likes of Thomas Reid ([1785] 2002) and Bernard Williams (1970), but I do not propose to develop a complete theory of personal identity here.

[3] I intend to argue for a positive answer to this question. This has also been done by Galen Strawson in *Freedom and Belief* (1986).

tell you "I know exactly what you mean. I wish I could talk to H. G. Wells." And then, of course, there are wishes for the merely impossible: take, for example, the wish never to have been born.

Faced with the distressed Pythagoras saying that he wishes the square root of two were rational, someone might say to him and our other individuals apparently wishing after the impossible, "No, you don't, really." What does this comment mean? Saying "You don't, really" in this context is not saying that one does not know one's own mental state—as in, "Deep down, you don't really wish to help me; you wish to feel like you are helping me." Nor is it always the same as telling a person that she has not thought through the implications, logical or empirical, of her wishes, as when we tell a person "You say you wish you had a horse, but believe me, you don't. Horses are very high maintenance animals and it would drive you crazy." The philosopher who wishes he could talk to H. G. Wells did, ex hypothesi, think through the question of the possibility of time travel, and came to the conclusion that it is incoherent. If you say "I wish I were Russell" and someone tells you, "Oh no, you don't; if you were Russell you would not be there to be Russell," we tend to respond with the words, "Come on, you know what I mean," and the person generally admits that she does.

If you "don't really" wish to be Russell, but one "knows what you mean," what is it that you mean? Let me start from an example that involves a more mundane sort of an impossible wish. Two events are about to take place simultaneously in two parts of the world; you find it very hard to decide which of them to attend, and you say "I wish I could be in two places at the same time." This is, one might claim, only an impossible thing, not an incoherent thing; but it probably does not cohere at all with many other things we wish quite strongly. You do not, for example, truly wish that the laws of physics would change in such a radical manner as would allow you to be in two places at the same time—you might believe that such a situation would be horrible in many ways. Still, it seems that you wish to be at two places at the same time, and to *also* wish for the laws of physics to stay the same. At times, you even feel as if you very much wish that you could be in two places at the same time. You feel that way because, whichever event you attend, it will pain you significantly not to have attended the other one. In fact, the amount of pain entailed by each choice might appear to be equal, and so your decision becomes difficult. It might even be that the more you think of the implications of your decision, the harder it is for you to make it.

It might be tempting to say that what I truly regret is simply the fact that the two events are on the same date. But it need not even be true that

I have this regret, much less that it is the only regret I have. We can imagine a person who *wants* the two events to be at the same time—perhaps she finds it wonderfully symbolic that her brother's birthday and the Gay Pride March fall on the same day—but who still has desires that could be fulfilled only if she could be in both places at the same time, and thus, in the sense I have discussed earlier, regrets that she could not be in two places at the same time.

Let us look again at a person who has to make a decision due to "not being able to be in two places at the same time." This person, I have said, might find herself in a state in which no matter what she would do, she is bound to have regrets of some sort. Some authors would suggest that in such a case, a case in which a decision leaves equally painful residue whatever alternative one chooses, one decides between two things that are incomparable (e.g., Griffin 1998; Raz 1998; Stocker 1998). They would especially be inclined to suggest that in cases where the stakes are high a person, for example, has to decide between an alternative in which she would spend more time with her children and an alternative in which she would devote most of her time to her work. Two of the things that make the thought appealing are the following. First, if the choice is psychologically difficult, mind-boggling in the more trivial cases, and downright tragic in some extreme cases, and if it seems in some sense to be legitimately or understandably difficult, it does not seem far fetched that there is also something conceptually special about it. Second, when a person attempts to decide between, say, being a lawyer and being a musician, it is very hard to come up with an algorithm or a practical reasoning manual that would tell him what to do. But the psychological difficulty involved in a decision—even the psychological difficulty that is understandable or expected in a person who makes a decision—is not a reliable sign that there is anything conceptually unusual about it, and the fact that it is impossible to come up with good advice as to how to choose between two alternatives does not mean that they cannot be comparable—and approximately equal, or, as Ruth Chang (1998) would have, on a par. This is so because when it comes to matters that are more complex than deciding between two sums of money or two ice-cream cones, deciding between two equal things can be a very difficult affair, and even deciding between two things, one of which is clearly better, can be rather painful.

Consider an example borrowed from Chang (1998, 23): Dave is trying to choose between being a lawyer and being a musician. He finds both alternatives attractive; in each case he finds that he would be pained to forgo the other alternative. Those who say that Dave is choosing between incomparable alternatives say that:

1. If Dave's decision between being a lawyer and being a musician were a choice between equal things, it would not be painful.
2. If Dave's decision between being a lawyer and being a musician were a choice between equal things, it would be true that if, say, one added a $1,000 to the Dave's salary as a lawyer, the decision would become straightforward, and he could, with no second thought, become a lawyer.
3. But Dave's decision is painful and difficult, and most of us in his place would not wish to solve it by flipping a coin, or find it possible to do so. If offered a life as a lawyer and a life as a musician, Dave's decision between them would not become simplified if the genie who makes the offer were to add, say, a $1,000 to Dave's prospective salary as a lawyer.

Therefore:

4. It cannot be the case that Dave's decision is a decision between equal things.

It seems to me that one assumes here that a decision between comparable things is as simple as a decision between two sums of money, and therefore can never legitimately inspire regret. If one wants money and has to choose between two sums of money, one chooses the larger one. If the sums are equal, one flips a coin or otherwise chooses randomly: it does not matter, other things being equal, if I accept the $1,000 dollars offered to me by Jason or the $1,000 dollars offered to me by John. Therefore, a decision between comparable things is a decision that ought to be a breeze: either one painlessly goes for the higher bid, or if the bids are equal, one painlessly tosses a coin. But I see no reason to think that all decisions between comparable things are as easy as decisions between sums of money. Let us note first that there are some decisions that are in a clear sense as straightforward (in the sense of one alternative being the more rational one) as a decision between $100 and $105, but which, unlike the monetary decision, leave behind painful longings. It is often clearly rational for a person to decide to escape a country in which he is in danger of persecution or oppression by a totalitarian regime, and the person who makes that decision often has no doubt as to what to do and, after the fact, never wishes to undo the past. However, it is quite common for such a person to spend many days longing painfully for the language, culture, music, or weather of the country he fled. A person might often regret never being able to experience special things that she has experienced with a past lover and which would be impossible to have with anyone else, but still be quite sure that her decision to break up and start her current relationship was the right decision. Naturally, both of these people can tell themselves not to be silly and to be happy with what they have—they might, overall, be happy with what they have. Painful feelings are not the same as regretting the decision itself. The point is that a person who chooses between $100 and $105 rarely experiences *any* painful longings upon recollecting the lost $100, but the person who chooses to leave the country or the lover often has some, and her belief that she has made the overall best choice does not completely get rid of these.

Here is one important difference between a choice between two sums of money and a choice between two more complex alternatives, one of which is nonetheless clearly better than the other. If one has to choose between $100 and $105, it is usually true that every need that can be satisfied with $100 can also be satisfied by $105. Things are different with the decisions above. Even if the second relationship is clearly better than the first relationship, it is usually false that every desire that can be satisfied by the first relationship can also be satisfied by the second one. Similarly, the person who flees persecution might have some deep desires and concerns that can be satisfied only in his country of origin—say, a great love of the literature and songs written in the country's language—and while going to a different, freer country might satisfy *more* of the person's concerns and desires, the love of the lost literature and language does not become extinguished just because the other desires have been satisfied. This does not make the two alternatives—staying in the country or leaving it—incomparable, as the person might vehemently and plausibly insist that he prefers being alive and full of longings to being dead or tortured, and that one alternative is therefore clearly better than the other. Still, while going is obviously better than staying, it is simply false that every desire that can be satisfied by staying can also be satisfied by going. And whenever a desire is left unsatisfied, some pain is likely to occur.

So, even in clear choices, some wistful longing might result. It sometimes happens, though, that a person cares about or desires very deeply things that cannot, for some reason or another, be achieved together. I am talking about cases in which there is no irrationality in having both concerns or desires. There is nothing irrational about having both desires that are best satisfied in the life of a musician and desires that are best satisfied in the life of a lawyer, nothing irrational about wanting your children to have the best possible upbringing *and* wanting ideal career performance: it just happens that, given facts about the world, it might be impossible to achieve both goals. In some cases—such as Dave's—the two lives might be on a par with regard to their value to the agent: each of the possible alternative involves a realization of some of Dave's values to the effect that an approximately equal measure of Dave's deeper desires will be satisfied and frustrated whatever choice he makes. Because the desires in question are different ones, I say they are "on a par" or "approximately equal," because, especially given the complexity of the world, a certain vagueness is inevitable here, and so adding $1,000 to the lawyer's prospective salary or an extra small gig to the musician's prospective career would not make Dave's decision any easier. However, there is no need to jump from "approximately equal values" to "incomparable values," because in many cases, adding $1 million to one of the prospective lives *would* make a difference.

It is true, too, that in some such cases it would be considered inappropriate to flip a coin. Note, though, that is not true for all of these cases. If Dave, having reasoned to the limits of his abilities, decides to flip a coin to decide whether to be a musician or a lawyer, or, more realistically, to accept the first scholarship offer that comes his way, whether it is in law or music, nothing seems particularly wrong with it, though if I were Dave, I would prefer to either discover, after a lot of thinking, that one alternative is better for me after all or to have something happen (say, meet a new girlfriend who prefers musicians to lawyers or vice versa) that would tip the scales. Coin tosses appear inappropriate in cases of particularly grave decisions that involve the fates of others. In these cases, assuming that rather than tossing a coin in lieu of thinking, one reasoned to the limit of one's abilities about the decision before being stymied, I think that a coin toss is inappropriate in the same way that laughing while discussing such matters is inappropriate—not because, strictly speaking, it is wrong but because, given what we know of human nature, a person who does not, in such circumstances, feel too emotionally wretched for a "heads or tails" attitude is most likely a person who is not appropriately concerned about morally important things. A parent who does not ever worry about a child seems strangely uncaring even if, in fact, there is no reason whatsoever to worry about the child: a romantic partner might seem as if he is not in love anymore if, in some situation, he feels no trace of jealousy, even though there is no reason for jealousy. Similarly, a person who plays a certain causal role in the killing of a fellow human being or in the causation of suffering appears not to be very morally concerned if he does not feel anguish—even if he has done nothing wrong. At any rate, I see no contradiction in believing that all human beings are equal in terms of the value of their life and finding it jarring to toss a coin in a life boat.

Let us go back to the state of wanting to be at two places at the same time. You care about music and you care about justice; you want to give your children the best possible upbringing and you want to pursue excellence in your art or sport, which seems to require working constantly; you want to be there for a good friend's wedding and you want not to miss a rare opportunity to go on a free trip to Antarctica. There is nothing particularly wrong with having both your desires, but it so happens that given all kinds of contingent facts, your wishes could not all be granted unless somehow the laws of physics were different. And so, as you say, "I wish I could be in two places at the same time," you express irritation at the arbitrary laws of nature, at the fact that they do not allow you to have what you want. Thus, there is one sense in which I find it reasonable (or at least not unreasonable) to wish for the ability to be in two places at the same time: it is not unreasonable to have a lot of individual things that you wish were the case or that you regret not having been the case, even though, it so happens, they could not be the case unless you could be in two places at the same time. "I wish I could be at two places at the same time" is generally the lament we make when this is the situation.

But if human beings are as subjected to the laws of nature as other things, if Nagelian freedom is impossible, than one can find oneself frustrated not with geographic facts, but with psychological facts. One might have strong desires that cannot be satisfied unless the laws of one's own psychology could somehow be bypassed. One can become frustrated with the laws that govern one's own psyche, and thus with one's inability to change them or ignore them, which amounts to being frustrated with the fact that one's psyche is, strictly speaking, governed by any natural laws at all, as opposed to being completely constituted by one's will. While few of us truly expect the laws of the outside world to comply with our wishes, the realization that even in the absence of anything like compulsion or psychosis, one's mind can be only marginally more pliable than other sections of the world can be particularly galling. Just as, in some situations, we have wishes that, though reasonable in themselves, could come true together only if it were possible to be in two places at the same time or to live twice or to travel in time, we also have desires that could come true together only if we were not stuck with some of our beliefs, desires, values, and other mental qualities, and with the laws of psychology, about as much as we are stuck with our bodies and with the laws of biology.

Naturally, we are not completely stuck with all of our physical attributes. But often we expect more freedom with regard to our minds. No one thinks that by thinking alone, or by an act of will alone, one can gain muscle, lose fat, or change the shape of one's lips. On the other hand, we are forever haunted by the mirage of controlling our minds by sheer act of will. This is partially because we can will mental *acts*, like deliberating and imagining, just as easily as we can will physical *act*s, such as raising an arm. But just as we cannot directly will our height or weight, we cannot will into existence, or out of existence, desires, or beliefs, or concerns, or values. If one wants to cause oneself to stop caring about what one's father thinks, stop loving the man or woman one can't have, or stop worrying and learn to love the bomb, one cannot simply will one's love or worry or reverence out of existence. One has to embark on a project, as difficult as molding a physical object (though whether the comparable object is clay or marble varies with the individual case). To change anything of that sort you will have to engage with the laws of nature just as carefully as an engineer—either in a blatant form by taking a drug or in form of laborious cunning around your psychology.

Note that even such a project will often face a problem that is not involved in shaping physical objects: the person who tries to change her desires and beliefs is herself the bundle of desires and beliefs that she wants to change. This creates at least two further potential problems. Perhaps the more obvious one is the creation of "blind spots." I, for example, have yet to bring myself to stop being superstitious in a "knock on wood" kind of way, because I cannot help feeling that if I start embarking on a superstition-elimination project, I would jinx myself. A very narcissistic person might likewise fail to become a better person simply because he cannot even imagine what an unselfish person is like, and a romantic person might be so romantic as to pursue becoming levelheaded in a way that is too romantic for her goal. A person who wants to become less pessimistic can of course underestimate his chances of successfully doing so, and a person who is arrogant can be too arrogant about her chances to become less so. A more subtle problem arises from the fact that while you cannot will beliefs and desires out of existence, the very fact that you have a desire to change changes the thing that you want to change—in a way that is either favorable or not so. The bad person who wants to be good generally becomes at least somewhat less bad as a result of that very desire. On the other hand, a very nervous person who develops a desire to stop being nervous might become somewhat more nervous as a result. These problems arising from motivation and introspection make it true that human beings are quite bad at assessing their ability to change things about themselves, and thus my view that self-change is difficult does not imply that one should despair of it. If anything, it implies that one should go about it in more sophisticated ways than New Year's resolutions, which is hardly a new claim.

But the cases I most wish to discuss here are cases in which self-change projects might never come into question, because they are, in Frankfurt's sense, unthinkable. I do not wish to discuss here traditional cases of akrasia—cases in which one tries to get rid of an obnoxious urge, like the urge to smoke, which one does not value. I am thinking here of cases in which one genuinely values something—as in Frankfurtian volitional necessity cases—but also is bitterly sad about this. Perhaps this is one way to imagine the predicament described by Dorothy Parker in the following poem, "Love Song":

> My own dear love, he is strong and bold
> And he cares not what comes after.
> His words ring sweet as a chime of gold,
> And his eyes are lit with laughter.
> He is jubilant as a flag unfurled—
> Oh, a girl, she'd not forget him.
> My own dear love, he is all my world,—
> And I wish I'd never met him.

The speaker in this poem need not necessarily be talking about sheer physical attraction or silly teenaged romance. She might truly love the person in question, truly value him and care for him, but her love of him might have caused her so much hardship, perhaps cost her so many other things that she truly values, that she might wish she never had to be introduced to this particular value. She might love the man in question too much to try to release herself from him—and in a way, regret that too, feeling trapped within herself.

Imagine a person who, like Thomas Moore in *A Man for All Seasons*, values telling the truth above all else. One day, he faces the choice of telling a lie or being executed. He values the truth so much that he chooses to tell it anyway, thus facing the prospect of being executed. It is quite possible to imagine this person, without wavering the slightest bit from his tragic decision, wishing that he did not care about the truth *quite this much* (which is, after all, a fairly extreme, arguably supererogatory amount). He might wish that he could turn off or "tone down" his concern for the truth for just this occasion. But of course, he cannot do it—he can do no other— and so wishing that he could tone down his concern for the truth for the occasion is de facto a wish to step out of himself—to have a self that is separate from the chunk of beliefs and desires moving itself inexorably toward death—and to tweak his mental states, just a bit, so as to make his situation less unbearable.

Because however much he might care about the truth above all else, he cares, presumably, about many other things—and about some of them almost as much. He wants to live for the reasons other people want to live, and just as badly. Perhaps he cares very much about his friends or family, and if he dies, they are likely to suffer immense difficulties, even apart from emotional devastation. Perhaps he has other ideals and passions beyond truth, only it so happens that truth is the one that got him into trouble. And most likely, there is no inner contradiction between valuing the truth and valuing the other things he values. Only accidental circumstances made them conflict. The exact details do not matter here. The point is that one can have a set concerns that can only be accommodated if one were not the sort of person who values the truth above all else, *and* at same time, value the truth above all else.

Some romantic souls would be tempted to tell the person in question something like, "You would not want it any other way. After all, actions speak louder than words, and look what you chose." We might even fail to be convinced if he answers, "But wait, I can't want it any other way, but at the moment *I wish I could*." But as we have seen earlier, deciding between things that you value is not like deciding between sums of money, even if the decision is straightforward (albeit psychologically painful) for the person who makes it. A person who accepts an offer of $1,000 while rejecting an offer of $900 would not generally complain. If he complains about the fact that he could not have accepted both offers together, we would—unless he is badly in need—tell him to stop whining. But we cannot say "stop whining" to the person whose concern for the truth makes it necessary for him to sacrifice everything (else) that is dear to him.

Our truth seeker cannot tell the lie while at the same time, as Frankfurt would put it, be who he is. Thus he can, at the same time, feel that not telling a lie would be the right thing to do *and* experience his inability to tell the lie as something resembling akrasia. Sure, it is the right thing to do, but why, for God's sake, is he the one who always has to do the right thing? This is the sort of situation in which a person, though being, both objectively and in her own experience, "her true self" can still experience that very self as constraining, as forcing things on her. This is where a person might wish for Sartrean or Nagelian freedom—a freedom to decide who to be. And while his wish would be at least as crazy as a wish for the ability to pull oneself up by one's own bootstraps or to be in two places at once, it would also be, in a similar way, understandable. It is like a wish for a miracle. Some of us are much more prone than others to wishing for miracles, but perhaps in this particular sense, there are no naturalists in the trenches.

Bibliography

Alston, W. P. 1993. "Epistemic Desiderata." *Philosophy and Phenomenological Research* 53 (3): 527–51.

American Psychiatric Association. 2000. *Diagnostic and Statistical Manual-IV-TR.*

Anscombe, E. 1969. *Intention.* Ithaca: Cornell University Press.

Armstrong, L., with S. Jenkins. 2003. *Every Second Counts.* New York: Broadway Books.

Armstrong, L., and S. Jenkins. 2001. *It's Not About the Bike.* New York City, New York: Berkley Publishing Group.

Arpaly, N. 2003. *Unprincipled Virtue.* Oxford: Oxford University Press.

Arpaly, N., and T. Schroeder. 1999. "Praise, Blame, and the Whole Self." *Philosophical Studies* 93:161–88.

Ayer, A. J. [1954] 1980. "Freedom and Necessity." In *Philosophical Essays.* Westport, Conn.: Greenwood Press Reprint.

Bok, H. 1998. *Freedom and Responsibility.* Princeton: Princeton University Press.

Carnegie, Dale. 1981. *How to Win Friends and Influence People.* New York: Pocket Books.

Chang, R. 1997. "Introduction." In R. Chang, ed., *Incommensurability, Incomparability, and Practical Reason.* Cambridge: Harvard University Press.

Chisholm, R. 1978. "Comments and Replies." *Philosophia* 7:622–23.

Churchland, P. S. 1996. "Feeling Reasons." In A. Damasio, H. Damasio, and Y. Christen, eds., *Neurobiology of Decision-Making*, 181–99. Berlin: Springer-Verlag.

Clarke, R. 2003. *Libertarian Accounts of Free Will.* Oxford: Oxford University Press.

Copp, D. 1995. "'Ought' Implies 'Can', Blameworthiness, and the Principle of Alternate Possibilities." In D. Widerker and M. McKenna, eds., *Moral Responsibility and Alternative Possibilities.* Burlington, Vt.: Ashgate, 2003.

Cox, L. 2004. *Swimming to Antarctica: Tales of a Long-Distance Swimmer.* New York: Knopf.

Damasio, A. 1994. *Descartes' Error: Emotion, Reason, and the Human Brain.* New York: Putnam.

Davidson, D. 1980. "Actions, Reasons, and Causes." In *Essays on Actions and Events.* Oxford: Oxford University Press.

Dennett, Daniel. 1984. *Elbow Room: The Varieties of Free Will Worth Wanting.* Cambridge, Mass.: Bradford Books.

Dretske, F. 1988. *Explaining Behavior.* Cambridge: MIT Press.

Dworkin, G. 1970. "Acting Freely." *Nous* 4:367–83.

Feldman, M., C. Ford, and T. Reinhold. 1995. *Patient or Pretender: Inside the Strange World of Factitious Disorders.* Hoboken, N.J.: John Wiley and Sons.

Fischer J., and M. Ravizza. 1998. *Responsibility and Control: A Theory of Moral Responsibility*. New York: Cambridge University Press.

Frankfurt, H. 1999. *Autonomy, Volition, and Love*. Cambridge: Cambridge University Press.

———. 1988. *The Importance of What We Care About*. Cambridge: Cambridge University Press.

———. 1971. "Freedom of the Will and the Concept of a Person." *Journal of Philosophy* 68:5–20.

———. 1969. "Alternate Possibilities and Moral Responsibility." *Journal of Philosophy* 66:829–39.

Gilliam, Terry, director. 1975. *Monty Python and the Holy Grail*. Columbia Tri Star.

Ginet, C. 1990. *On Action*. Cambridge: Cambridge University Press.

Griffin, J. 1997. "Incommensurability: What's the Problem?" "In R. Chang, ed., *Incommensurability, Incomparability, and Practical Reason*. Cambridge: Harvard University Press.

Haji, I. 2002. *Deontic Morality and Control*. Cambridge: Cambridge University Press.

———. 1998. *Moral Appraisability: Puzzles, Proposals, and Perplexities*. New York: Oxford University Press.

Honderich, T. 2002. *How Free Are You? The Determinism Problem*. Oxford: Oxford University Press.

Hookway, C. 2000. "Epistemic Norms and Theoretical Deliberation." In J. Dancy, ed. *Normativity*, 60–77. Oxford: Blackwell.

Kane, R. 1998. *The Significance of Free Will*. Oxford: Oxford University Press.

Kant, I. 1964. *Groundwork for the Metaphysics of Morals*. Translated by H. Patton. New York: Harper and Row.

Kim, J. 2000. *Mind in a Physical World: An Essay on the Mind-Body Problem and Mental Causation*. Cambridge, Mass.: Bradford Books.

Korsgaard, C. 1996. *The Sources of Normativity*. Cambridge: Cambridge University Press.

Kramer, P. 1993. *Listening to Prozac*. New York: Viking.

Lazar, A. 1999. "Deceiving Oneself or Self-Deceived? On the Formation of Beliefs 'under the Influence.' " *Mind* 108:265–90.

Le Carré, J. 2004. *Little Drummer Girl*. New York: Scribner's.

Le Doux, J., and E. Phelps. 2000. "Emotional Networks in the Brain." In M. Lewis and J. Haviland-Jones, eds., *Handbook of Emotions*, 2d ed., 157–72. New York: Guilford Press.

Lehrer, K. 1990. *Metamind*. New York: Oxford University Press.

Locke, J. [1690] 1994. *An Essay Concerning Human Understanding*. New York: Prometheus Books.

Marlowe, A. 1999. *How to Stop Time*. New York: Anchor Books.

Mele, A. 2003. *Motivation and Agency*. Oxford: Oxford University Press.

———. 2000. *Self-Deception Unmasked*. Princeton: Princeton University Press.

———. 1995. *Autonomous Agents: From Self-Control to Autonomy*. Oxford: Oxford University Press.

Nabokov, V. 1991. *The Annotated Lolita*. New York: Random House.

Nagel, T. 1986. *The View from Nowhere*. Oxford: Oxford University Press.

———. 1982. "Moral Luck." In G. Watson, ed., *Free Will*, 174–86. New York: Oxford University Press.

Neely, W. 1974. "Freedom and Desire." *Philosophical Review* 83:32–54.

O'Conner, T. 2000. *Persons and Causes*. Oxford: Oxford University Press.

Parfit, D. 1986. *Reasons and Persons*. Oxford: Oxford University Press.

———. 1971. "Personal Identity." *Philosophical Review*, 80:3–27.

Pereboom, D. 2001. *Living without Free Will*. Cambridge: Cambridge University Press.

Petit, P., and M. Smith. 1990. "Backgrounding Desire." *Philosophical Review* 91: 565–92.

Raz, J. 1998. "Incommensurability and Agency." In R. Chang, ed., *Incommensurability, Incomparability, and Practical Reason*. Cambridge: Harvard University Press.

Reid, T. [1785] 2002. *Essays on the Intellectual Powers of Man*. University Park: Pennsylvania State University Press.

Sacks, O. 1987. *The Man Who Mistook His Wife for a Hat*. New York: Harper Perrenial.

Schillier, F. [1793] 1983. *On the Aesthetic Education of Man*. Oxford: Oxford University Press.

Schroeder, T. Forthcoming. "Moral Responsibility and Tourette Syndrome." *Philosophy and Phenomenological Research*.

Searle, J. 1980. "Minds, Brains, and Programs." *Behavioral and Brain Sciences* 3:417–57.

Sehon, S. 1997. "Deviant Causal Chains and the Irreducibility of Teleological Explanations." *Pacific Philosophical Quarterly* 78:196–213.

Sher, G. 2001. "Blame for Traits." *Noûs* 35 (1): 146–61.

Sinnott-Armstrong, W. 1984. "Ought Conversationally Implies Can." *Philosophical Review* 93:241–61.

Smart, J.J.C., and B. Williams. 1973. *Utilitarianism: For and Against*. Cambridge: Cambridge University Press.

Smith, M. 1994. *The Moral Problem*. Oxford: Blackwell.

Spinoza, B. [1674] 1995. Letter 58. In *The Letters* Indianapolis: Hackett Publishing Company.

Steup, M., ed. 2001. *Knowledge, Truth, and Duty*. Oxford: Oxford University Press.

Stocker, M. 1998. "Abstact and Concrete Value: Plurality, Conflict, and Maximization." In R. Chang, ed., *Incommensurability, Incomparability, and Practical Reason*. Cambridge: Harvard University Press.

Strawson, G. 1986. *Freedom and Belief*. Oxford: Oxford University Press.

Strawson, P. 1962. "Freedom and Resentment." *Proceedings of the British Academy* 48:1–25.

Stump, E. 1988. "Sanctification and Free Will." *Journal of Philosophy* 85:395–420.

Thomson, J. J. 1971. "A Defense of Abortion." *Philosophy and Public Affairs* 1:47–66.

van Inwagen, P. 1975. "The Incompatibility of Free Will and Determinism." *Philosophical Studies* 27:185–99.

Velleman, J. D. 1992. "What Happens When Someone Acts?" *Mind* 101:461–81.

Wallace, J. 1994. *Responsibility and the Moral Sentiments.* Cambridge: Harvard University Press.

Watson, Gary. 1996. "The Two Faces of Responsibility." *Philosophical Topics* 24: 227–48.

———. 1993. "Responsibility and the Limits of Evil: Variations on a Strawsonian Theme." In J. Fischer and M. Ravizza, eds., *Perspectives on Moral Responsibility,* 119–50. Ithaca N.Y.: Cornell University Press, 1993.

Watson, G. 1977. "Skepticism about Weakness of Will." *Philosophical Review* 86:316–39.

Whiteman, T., N. Novotni, and R. Peterson. 1995. *Adult ADD.* Colorado Springs, Colo.: Pinon Press.

Williams, B. 1981."Internal and External Reasons." In *Moral Luck.* New York: Cambridge University Press.

———. 1970. "The Self and the Future." *Philosophical Review.* 79(2):161–80.

Wilson, G. 1997. "Reasons as Causes *for* Action." In G. Holmstöm-Hintikka and R. Tuomela, eds, *Contemporary Action Theory.* Dordrecht: Kluwer.

Wolf, S. 1993a. "The Importance of Free Will." In J. Fischer and M. Ravizza, eds., *Perspectives on Moral Responsibility,* 101–18. Ithaca, N.Y.: Cornell University Press.

———. 1993b. "The Real Self View." In J. Fischer and M. Ravizza, eds., *Perspectives on Moral Responsibility,* 151–70. Ithaca, N.Y.: Cornell University Press.

———. 1980. "Asymmetrical Freedom." *Journal of Philosophy* 77:151–66.

Index

Sinnot-Armstrong, W, 107n.6
Smart, J.J.C., 11
Smith, Michael, 66
Spinoza, B., 86–87n
Steup, Mattias, 93–94
Stockholm Syndrome, 114
Strawson, Galen, 127n.3
Strawson, Peter: on good/ill will, 15;
    on reactive attitudes, 5, 6, 9, 11, 25
suppressing evidence, 98

technologies, changing, 109–10
temperament, 32
Thomson, J. J., 110
thought control, 97
time travel, altering the past through,
    127–28
Tourette Syndrome, 80, 81
tradition, sense of, 118–19
twelve-step programs, 119

van Inwagen, Peter, 37–38, 39,
    86, 91
Velleman, J. D., 23
virtues, 13, 104–6
volitional necessity, 42, 124–27

warrant: conceptions of, 10, 10n.2; vs.
    desirability, 9–13; and emotions, 36; of
    moral praise/blame, 13–17, 15nn.5–6,
    35–36
Washington, George, 4
Watson, G., 23
Watson, Gary, 33–34
The White House Mess (Buckley), 24
Wilde, Oscar, 56
Williams, Bernard, 67
wishful thinking, 74, 76, 100–101, 104,
    105–6
Wolf, Susan, 12, 34n.12, 42–43, 64
Woolf, Virginia, 40